Gordon R. DICKSON

a primary and secondary bibliography

Masters of
Science Fiction and Fantasy

Editor
L. W. Currey

Advisory Acquisitions Editor
Marshall B. Tymn

Other bibliographies in the series:

Lloyd Alexander, Evangeline Walton Ensley, and Kenneth Morris
Leigh Brackett, Marion Zimmer Bradley, and Anne McCaffrey
Samuel R. Delany
Ursula K. Le Guin
Andre Norton
Clifford D. Simak
Theodore Sturgeon
Jules Verne
Jack Williamson
Roger Zelazny

Gordon R. DICKSON
a primary and secondary bibliography

RAYMOND H. THOMPSON

G.K.HALL&CO.

70 LINCOLN STREET, BOSTON, MASS.

Library of Congress Cataloging in Publication Data

Thompson, Raymond H. (Raymond Henry), 1941-
    Gordon R. Dickson : a primary and secondary bibliog-
raphy.

    (Masters of science fiction and fantasy)
    Includes indexes.
    1. Dickson, Gordon R.—Bibliography.   I.   Title.
II.   Series.
Z8230.8.T47   1983   016.813'54   82-12126
[PS3554.I328]
ISBN 0-8161-8363-5

Contents

The Author

Raymond H. Thompson is currently Associate Professor of English at Acadia University, Wolfville, Nova Scotia, where he teaches medieval literature and fantasy and science fiction literature. A graduate of Queen's University, Belfast, Northern Ireland, he holds an M.A. from the University of Michigan and a Ph.D. from the University of Alberta. He has published a number of articles on science fiction and fantasy and on Arthurian literature, both in the medieval and modern periods.

Preface

Included in this bibliography are all the works published by
Gordon R. Dickson up to early 1981 that are listed in standard in-
dexes, such as Norm Metcalf, The Index of Science Fiction Magazines
1951-1965 (El Cerrito, Calif.: Stark, 1968); Erwin S. Strauss, The
MIT Science Fiction Society's Index to the S-F Magazines, 1951-1965
(Cambridge, Mass.: MIT Science Fiction Society, 1965) and continua-
tions compiled by the New England Science Fiction Association; William
Contento, Index to Science Fiction Anthologies and Collections (Boston:
G.K. Hall, 1978): and in annual editions of Books in Print in the
United States, Britain, and the European countries covered in Appendix
D.

This search has been supplemented by a check of the Dickson Papers
held in the University of Minnesota Libraries (see Appendix A) and of
the author's own collection and records. Also included are works of
criticism noted in "The Year's Scholarship in Science Fiction and
Fantasy," compiled annually in Extrapolation, by Roger C. Schlobin
and Marshall B. Tymn, and reviews listed in H.W. Hall, Science Fiction
Book Review Index, 1923-1973 (Detroit: Gale Research, 1975), and its
annual supplements; in standard indexes such as the annual Book Review
Index (Detroit: Gale Research); and in more specialized indexes such
as the annual New York Times Index. Reviews from newspapers collected
by the author or placed with the Dickson Papers have been added.

Critical material published too recently to appear in the latest
indexes may be excluded. Also excluded are guest of honor speeches
by or tributes to the author, which are published only in the program
booklets issued at science fiction conventions, and reviews in newspapers not listed in the indexes consulted or collected in the Dickson
Papers.

In order to verify the entries, I have examined the author's own
substantial collection of books and stories in magazines; the Dickson
Papers in the Manuscripts Division of the University of Minnesota
Libraries (see Appendix A); the Spaced-Out Library in Toronto, which
contains many British editions of books and a useful catalog of fanzines; the Walter A. Coslet Fanzine Collection at the University of

Preface

Maryland Library in Baltimore County; the MIT Science Fiction Society
Library, which houses the most extensive collection of foreign language magazines in North America (see Appendix D); and the Science
Fiction and Fantasy Collection of the Ward Chipman Library in the
University of New Brunswick (St. John). These trips were made possible by grants from the Harvey T. Reid Summer Study Fund at Acadia
University, Wolfville, Nova Scotia. Items I was unable to locate for
examination are indicated by an asterisk preceding the entry number,
with the source of my information given in brackets.

I should like to thank the following individuals for their courtesy and assistance in my research: Dennis Abblit, curator of the
Science Fiction and Fantasy Collection at the Ward Chipman Library;
Jean Beveridge, interlibrary loans librarian at Acadia University;
Maureen Dwyer-Hirten, special collections librarian at the University
of Maryland Library, Baltimore County; Carl Hylin, president of the
MIT Science Fiction Society; Linda Lounsbury, Dickson's former office
manager; Alan Lathrop, curator of the Manuscripts Division, University
of Minnesota Libraries; Andrew Malec, who prepared the inventory of
the Dickson Papers; Doris Mehegan, librarian of the Spaced-Out Library;
science fiction critic Sandra Miesel; Sonya Schonwinck, who supplied
information on German translations; and Dave Wixon, Dickson's business
manager.

I wish also to express my gratitude to Mrs. Maude Dickson for her
patience and courtesy; to Joy Cavazzi for typing the manuscript with
her usual skill and good humor; to my children for keeping interrup-
tions to a minimum; to my wife, Hilary, for her unfailing support and
encouragement; and of course to Gordy himself, a charming and delightful person, as well as a fine writer.

Introduction

Gordon Rupert Dickson was born on 1 November 1923, in Edmonton, Alberta, the son of a mining engineer. Although his father, Gordon Dickson, Sr., was Australian-born, the Dickson family had lived in Nova Scotia for almost a century before his grandfather went to sea and eventually formed his own shipping company. Migration from Australia to Canada was, thus, a return to a land in which the family had already planted deep roots. As is revealed in The Ante-Room, the autobiography of Gordon's half-brother, Lovat (himself a distinguished author and publisher), the Dicksons had a strong sense of family tradition, traces of which can be discerned in Gordon Dickson's writings, particularly in his characterization of the Dorsai. Indeed, features of the family background of Donal Graeme, central hero of Dorsai! (1959 [A96]), bear more than a passing resemblance to those of the author. Dickson's Scotch-Irish ancestors, in their quest for religious freedom, migrated first to Connecticut, then to Nova Scotia, where they helped drive the French out of Acadia.

As a child growing up in western Canada and attending school in British Columbia, Dickson learned to love the majestic mountain ranges and the wide Pacific Ocean with its ever-changing moods. Both reappear in his writings as the lofty uplands of the planet Dorsai with their quiet coniferous forests, and the seas of the Robby Hoenig series (1960-1964 [A101, A134, A141]) and of Home from the Shore and its sequel, The Space Swimmers (1963, 1967 [A137, A162]). Gordon Dickson, Sr.'s first wife had died shortly after the family came to Canada, and he had remarried a young American schoolteacher. When her husband died, Maude Dickson decided to return to the United States, and along with her son, then aged 13, moved to Minnesota.

Dickson entered the University of Minnesota in 1939, at the age of fifteen, to study creative writing under such notable figures as Sinclair Lewis and Robert Penn Warren. He had already discovered fantasy and science fiction in 1938, in the pages of Astounding, Unknown, Startling, and Famous Fantastic Mysteries. But it was not until 1942, when Dickson joined the newly formed Minneapolis Fantasy Society, or MFS, that he became a full-fledged fan. The picture of

his activities at this time is revealed in the pages of the MFS
Bulletin (see entries C1-C3), which describe long nights spent talking, singing, and drinking with friends who shared his interests.
They met writers like Clifford Simak, Carl Jacobi, and Donald Wandrei;
they held quizzes and wrote stories; Dickson even managed to get involved in a feud with another fan and aspiring writer, Joe Fortier
(see entry C5); and for a while they traded lively insults in the
rival columns of fanzines.

This pattern, so typical of fandom, was rudely interrupted by the
demands of war. Dickson, who was a corporal in the Reserve Officers
Training Corps, was drafted in April 1943, and remained in the army
until 1946. Although he did not see active service, this was to prove
a valuable training for the aspiring author, since many of his early
stories explore how soldiers react under stress. The subject receives
its most extended treatment not only in the novels and tales of the
Dorsai, his interstellar mercenaries of the far future, but also in
Naked to the Stars (1961 (A123]), a fine study of the conflict between
the idealism and reality of warfare.

After the war, Dickson returned to the University of Minnesota,
where he completed his B.A. in 1948, with a major in creative writing,
and settled into graduate school. He helped reestablish the MFS, which
had lapsed soon after his departure, and served as secretary-treasurer.
The Society became more social in nature, engaging in activities such
as playing chess, singing ballads, and verbally building science fiction stories as they were passed around the table from one person to
another. Among the new members was Poul Anderson. The two became
fast friends and later collaborated on the Hoka stories.

In 1950, Dickson finally recognized that his prime interest lay
in writing, not teaching. He decided to leave graduate school, and,
as he puts it, "walked off the dock into the sea of freelance writing,
where for the next few years nothing much was to be seen of me but
frantic thrashings to keep my head above water and even more frantic
bubblings at times when my head was under the water" ("The Childe
Cycle," 1965 [C17]). It was a period when he survived on peanut butter sandwiches, supplemented by vitamins, and sold blood to supplement
his sporadic income.

Since those early days, Dickson, who continues to live in the Twin
Cities area, has risen to become one of the most respected and best-
loved writers in the field. He served two terms as president of the
Science Fiction Writers of America, from 1969-1971, and he remains one
of the most popular members on the speakers' circuit he helped to set
up. His encouragement and help to other writers, particularly younger
talents, has won the gratitude of authors like Kate Wilhelm, Spider
Robinson, Joe Haldeman, Robert Asprin, and Lynn Abbey. He has regularly participated in programs offered at the Milford Conferences and
the SF Institute at the University of Kansas. An enthusiastic launch
watcher, Dickson has drawn material from the space program for both

factual articles (see entry C28) and novels like <u>Gremlins, Go Home!</u>
(1974 [A195]) and <u>The Far Call</u> (1973 [A194]), the latter much praised
for its attention to realistic detail. Amidst these many interests
and demands upon his time, Dickson retains a capacity for enjoying
life that is proverbial. His friend Ben Bova even composed "The
Ballad of Gordy Dickson," set to the tune of "Clementine" and collected
in <u>NESFA Hymnal</u> (see entry B12), which pays him the tribute: "Science
Fiction is his hobby,/But his main job's having fun. . . . Always
eating, always drinking,/When the hell does Gordy write?"

Yet write he does, and with notable success. To date Dickson has
published 50 books (36 novels, 10 collections, and 4 edited anthologies), 161 pieces of shorter fiction, 9 radio plays, and a variety of
works that include poems, songs, letters, biographical sketches, reviews, critical articles, and texts of speeches. While he made a few
early forays into romantic fiction (see entries A3, A4, A6), westerns
(see entries A12, A29), and detective mysteries (see entries A108,
A116), he has concentrated upon science fiction and the related fields
of fantasy and supernatural horror. Dickson has written specifically
for juveniles, in the Robby Hoenig series and <u>Gremlins, Go Home!</u>; for
adolescents, in <u>Space Winners</u> and <u>Star Prince Charlie</u> (entries A154,
A201); as well as for young and old alike, in a whole range of works
that are frequently reviewed as adult fiction suitable for younger
readers.[1]

His writings have been widely translated (see Appendix D) and have
earned many awards: "Soldier, Ask Not" (A145) won a 1965 Hugo as best
short story; "Call Him Lord" (A158) the 1966 Nebula in the novelette
category; <u>The Dragon and the George</u> (A206) the British Fantasy Award
for best novel of 1976; "Time Storm" (A210) a Jupiter Award from the
Instructors of Science Fiction in Higher Education for best novelette
of 1977; "Lost Dorsai" (A225) the 1980 Hugo as best novella; "The
Cloak and the Staff" (A227) the 1980 Hugo as best novelette. Additionally, Dickson has received other honors, such as the First Annual
Stanley G. Weinberg Memorial Award for outstanding contributions to
the field of science fiction and fantasy, given in 1977 by the committee which ran X-Con, the first Milwaukee SF Convention, and the E.E.
Smith Memorial Award for Imaginative Fiction, also known as the
"Skylark," at Boston.

Like Smith, of whom he was an early admirer, Dickson is known for
his development of series (see Appendix C). The earliest was the Hoka
series, written in collaboration with his college friend, Poul
Anderson.[2] These tales of a race of lovable aliens, with a striking
resemblance to teddy bears and an insatiable love of imitation, parody
the cliches of various popular literary topics, such as the western,
the detective mystery, pirate adventure, the baseball sports yarn, and
Foreign Legion romance.

Probably the funniest is "In Hoka Signo Vinces" (1953 [A26]), in
which the Hokas decide to set up a space patrol "to scour the evildoer

from the stars." After an inspection that involves their leader's "touching the nose of each spaceman to see that it was cold and moist," the patrol sets off in a tiny courier boat, armed with primitive gunpowder cannon and revolvers; following a farcical sequence of events, the patrol succeeds in capturing a massive enemy battleship that is totally unprepared for dealing with such small unsophisticated weapons. The concept was later developed more fully by Anderson in his award-winning novel, The High Crusade; but here the emphasis falls upon humor, as the enemy admiral surrenders with the comment, much enjoyed by Damon Knight (see entry D9), "if turning on the fire extinguisher sprinklers, the fumigation system, the leak-detector smoke system, the emergency radionic-heating system, the emergency refrigeration system, and directing the sewers into the deck-flushing system isn't a dirty way to fight, I'd like to know what is."

One reason for the success of the Hoka series is its interesting use of role-playing: the Hokas manage to force others into the roles they have cast for them with uncanny skill and appropriateness, particularly in "Undiplomatic Immunity" (1959 [A69]). This is partly a narrative convenience, but it is also a penetrating comment upon the dymanics of human interaction. Moreover, as the bemused human protagonists struggle to cope with the unfamiliar role into which they have been cast, both the existing possibilities and unexpected dangers of developing unsuspected potential are increasingly explored as the series develops. This theme provides a serious underlying significance to Star Prince Charlie (1975 [A201]), the most recent collaboration and the first full-length Hoka novel.

Dickson's first independent series, dealing with the adventures of Tom and Lucy Parent, was much less successful. It makes some wry comments upon human reaction to aliens, but only when it adopts the Hoka pattern of forcing people into roles with comic results, in "The Faithful Wilf" (1963 [A139]), does it really come alive.

By then, however, Dickson had already started another series, about the planet Dilbia, in which he explored in greater depth the possibilities for developing untapped talents by forcing a character to adopt an unlikely role against his will. Parallels with the earlier series did not escape the critics, who described the huge, bear-like Dilbians as "Hokas grown up" (see entry D80), and noted the presence of the same confused and reluctant hero. Some also grumbled that the stories and novels merely repeated the same plot formula; they failed to appreciate how the author deepened his study of character adapting to unfamiliar demands by showing the importance of empathy in Spacepaw (1969 [A167]) and "The Law-Twister Shorty" (1971 [A180]).

1960, the year when the Dilbian series began, also saw the start of the Robby Hoenig series for juveniles. The strength of this latter lies in its informative use of the sea and its creatures, and the lesson it teaches about open-mindedness, though it does tend to lapse into didacticism. In a less serious vein are the stories of Hank

Introduction

Shallo, World Scout. The hero is a wily but irresponsible bachelor
who survives by his wits. While the situations are entertaining, they
sometimes seem contrived, always a danger in the kind of parody that
Dickson so enjoys. Shallo is a lighthearted figure who harks back to
the author's undergraduate days, and he has little potential for growth
without changing his very essence. He is last seen in "Catch a Tartar"
(1965 [A150]) heading out into deep space to evade responsibility in
the shape of a designing female. He is unlikely to return.

A more recent series of stories about Shane Everts, human trans-
lator for the supremely arrogant aliens who have conquered Earth so
effortlessly, shows the author in a more serious mood. The stories
reveal the endurance of the human spirit of hope despite overwhelming
odds. The subject is common enough in Dickson's works, but here it
is enhanced by powerful suspense. The series is destined to become a
novel when the author can find the time to complete the task.

In the meantime, his energies have been taken up with work on the
best-known of his series, the Childe Cycle. The roots of the cycle
are found in "Lulungomeena" (1954 [A34]), an ironic tale that introduces the figure of a battle-scarred veteran of the Dorsai planets;
a Dorsai mercenary is the narrator in "Act of Creation" (1957 [A68]);
finally, Dorsai! (1959 [A96]) introduces Donal Graeme, hero of the
cycle, and native of what has now become a single world known as The
Dorsai. The notion for this novel, which was runner-up for the Hugo
Award in 1960, was stimulated by Rafael Sabatini's Bellarion, and drew
upon ideas developed in The Pikeman, the unfinished historical novel
Dickson had begun while still a student (see Appendix A). However, it
was not until the Milford Conference in June 1960 that the concept of
the cycle was born. After talking the idea over with friend and fellow author Richard McKenna, Dickson arrived at a final outline that
has changed little since then.

The thematic argument of the cycle is that mankind is in the process
of evolving toward a condition that the author calls Responsible Man.
This ethical evolution started about the fourteenth century with the
Renaissance; it is now at the halfway stage and will be complete in
about another five hundred years. This next phase involved humanity's
splitting up into "Splinter Cultures," each of which specializes in a
particular direction. The three most important of these groups are
the warriors (Dorsai), philosophers (Exotics), and believers, or men
of faith (Friendlies). Each develops its own area of specialization
to a degree not otherwise possible, but all must eventually reunite
in order to complete the evolutionary step to becoming Responsible
Man.

In "Notes on the Childe Cycle" (1973 [C30]), Dickson describes
his plan to chronicle this evolution in three historical, three contemporary, and three "future historical," or science fiction novels,
"within a structure rather like that of a three-act play," each with
three scenes. The three science fiction novels have now been divided

into six, of which four have been completed: Dorsai! (1959 [A96], also published in a cut version as The Genetic General), Necromancer (1962 [A128], also published as None but Man), Soldier, Ask Not (1967 [A163]), and The Tactics of Mistake (1970 [A178]). Dickson is currently engaged in writing the final two novels, entitled The Final Encyclopedia and Childe.3 Additionally, the author has written four "Illuminations": "Warrior" (1965 [A157]), "Brothers" (1973 [A190]), "Amanda Morgan" (1979 [A222]), and "Lost Dorsai" (1980 [A225]). In these he focuses upon details within the cycle that he does not have space to develop in the major novels.

Dickson's plans for the historical stage have advanced to the point of selecting the hero for all three novels: Sir John Hawkwood, the fourteenth century English mercenary, is his warrior; John Milton, as propagandist and pamphleteer for Cromwell's government, is his man of faith; Robert Browning is his philosopher. Plans for the contemporary stage are less developed, but George Santayana will probably be the philosopher in the first novel.

Predictably, such an impressive undertaking has excited considerable attention. Readers have shown the strongest interest in the warrior Dorsai, a taste partly catered to by the author in his Illuminations, and the entire cycle is sometimes erroneously called the Dorsai series. Critics such as Sandra Miesel have pondered the plan both in concept and execution, and as understanding of the undertaking has grown, so has appreciation and approval. The main objections have focused upon what is perceived as flat characterization. This complaint arises out of a failure to appreciate Dickson's technique, for he himself has described the Childe Cycle as a "showpiece for the consciously thematic novel" (see entry C52).

This technique is part of the romance mode,4 and it requires that the subject be explored through external action. Elements of the human psyche are represented by the characters. The total interaction between these representative figures thus becomes a psychomachia. Internal development of the characters would destroy their representative role; what happens instead is that the characters grow into a fuller realization and control of the untapped potential they possess from the outset. Donal Graeme, hero of the cycle, does not develop from a Dorsai warrior type to become Responsible Man. This he has always been, as the opening line of Dorsai! makes clear: "The boy was odd." The introspection whose absence has been deplored (see entry D239) is of little use in the romance mode, except insofar as it clarifies the elements embodied by a character on this vast canvas. Not individuals, but Dickson's entire universe represents the complex, evolving personality of mankind. This accounts, too, for the power of the Childe Cycle. It is an ideal choice of subject for the particular literary technique that the author deploys with such unobtrusive skill. By contrast, his attempts to explore what one critic calls "inner space" (D117) in novels like Sleepwalkers World (1971 [A183]) and The Pritcher Mass (1972 [A187]) have been less successful, despite some powerful effects.[5]

Unfortunately, the attention commanded by this impressive cycle has cast Dickson's other writings into the shadow of critical neglect. This is doubly regrettable because the conflicting judgments expressed in reviews of his fiction suggest that the critical approach has been too casual. Apart from Sandra Miesel's perceptive study of Home from the Shore and The Space Swimmers (see entry D223), my own article on the appeal of Dickson's fiction to adolescents (see entry D254), and a few thoughtful reviews of individual novels, critical comments (though generally favorable) have tended to be highly subjective, fluctuating between careless dismissal and indiscriminate enthusiasm. Thus The R-Master is praised in one place as "Taut, fast-paced, thought provoking" (D127), elsewhere condemned for its labored plot, uninspired prose and ideas, and two-dimensional characters (D142); Time Storm is hailed in one review as the author's "best book to date" (D208), in another castigated as "a dishonest crock, episodic, and carelessly written" (D214). The reader may well be excused for wondering whether the reviewers are discussing the same book.

Part of the problem is that science fiction fandom is much given to likes and dislikes, a reaction fostered both by professional magazines that regularly publish readers' letters rating their stories, and by the proliferation of fanzines. While these outlets are valuable, particularly to aspiring writers, they do encourage the criterion of personal taste rather than balanced judgment, with the erratic results observed. Thus P. Walker condemns Ancient, My Enemy as forgetable and "badly written" (D161), but waxes lyrical over the virtues of The Far Call, which represents "the best sf has to offer literature" (D226). The latter may be the better of the two books, and the reviewer has undoubtedly gained experience in the three intervening years; yet one does suspect that personal preference for the impressive realism of the latter over the techniques of romance writing, which are evident in the former, significantly influences his judgment. The reader would do well to keep this factor in mind when assessing reviews of any science fiction author.

Certainly, a most important consideration in evaluating the work of any writer is to understand its context, and to this end it is useful to examine some of the more prominent features of Dickson's fiction. Of these, one of the most striking is the study of man's reaction under stress. As mankind ventures forth in the universe, he meets many challenges, and these serve as proving grounds for the human spirit. Against open antagonism that must be countered in battle, stories like "Steel Brother" (1952 [A14]), "The Invaders" (1952 [A19]), and "The Question" (1958 [A83]) extol the virtues of courage and tenacity, although a warning against blind obedience is given in "The Underground" (1955 [A54]). Even more probing are those personal duels that force the hero to dig down deeply into his own personality to find the will and resources to prevail. These have given rise to some of Dickson's most intense tales, such as "On Messenger Mountain" (1964 [A144]), "In

the Bone" (1966 [A159]), and "Ancient, My Enemy" (1969 [A171]). Very
similar in style are stories like "Tiger Green" (1965 [A155]) and
"Building on the Line" (1968 [A164]), in which alien assault upon the
human mind produces a skilfully created sense of delirium. In many
cases the hero succeeds by using his ingenuity to outwit his oppon-
ents, and this is the formula employed in the Hank Shallo series, as
well as in "The Star-Fool" (1951 [A13]) and "Turnabout" (1955 [A43]).
Yet he can outsmart himself, too, if he is not careful, as happens in
"The Monkey Wrench" (1951 [A11]). While the protagonists may be es-
sentially ordinary people learning to cope with a difficult situation,
as in "The Amateurs" (1961 [A117]) and "In Iron Years" (1974 [A199]),
more commonly they discover extraordinary powers and abilities, as in
"Danger--Human!" (1957 [A77]), "The Game of Five" (1960 [A103]), and
in novels like Wolfling (1969 [A166]), Hour of the Horde (1969 [A169]),
and Time Storm (1977 [A213]).

Placing man in a situation of stress not only proves his resource-
fulness, but also raises questions about the issue of responsibility.
This becomes central in the Childe Cycle, but it is widespread through-
out Dickson's work. Early stories like "Ricochet on Miza" (1952
[A15]), "Itco's Strong Right Arm" (1954 [A38]), and "It Hardly Seems
Fair" (1960 [A104]), as well as a later novelette like Pro (1975
[A204]), all show ruthless and ambitious men ironically "hoist by
their own petard." Where the exploitation is conducted under the
guise of group or racial loyalty, however, as in Naked to the Stars,
Home from the Shore, and The Masters of Everon (1979 [A220]), the
criticism grows more incisive and far-reaching. Man's problem, as
Dickson perceives it, is a lack of sensitivity to the needs of others,
which leads to disaster in "An Honorable Death" (1961 [A115]) when the
alien natives avenge past wrongs by massacring the "superior" humans.
The solution to this insensitivity, the author argues in "Listen"
(1952 [A17]) and "Twig" (1974 [A197]), is empathy. One must reach
out and try to understand others, as happens in "Black Charlie" (1954
[A35]).

Consideration of this advice leads one to what emerges as the most
pervasive theme in Dickson's works, namely, the conflict between illusion and reality. This conflict emerges most clearly when we scruti-
nize the figure of the alien in Dickson's writings. From the very
outset, his aliens have attracted critical admiration: reviewers of
his first novel, Alien from Arcturus (1956 [A55]), found little to ex-
cite their enthusiasm with the exception of Peep, praised by Damon
Knight as a "furiously gentle creature of comic dignity" (see entry
D2; cf. entries D4, D5). The term "comic dignity" not only aptly describes many of the aliens who occupy Dickson's universe, but indi-
cates their essential paradox. What the human protagonists in these
stories have to learn is that behind their comic appearance lie qual-
ities of great worth. At the conclusion of Alien from Arcturus, the
humans learn that their alien friend, whom they consider "the most un-
worldly, and impractical screwball that ever was," is really an emin-
ent intergalactic authority in his field of research and ultimately

the individual who wins for Earth admission into the Galactic
Federation. Peep reappears in Space Winners (1965 [A154]) to teach
a trio of youngsters from Earth that initial reactions to situations
can be mistaken.

The Hokas can be similarly underestimated, as strangers learn to
their cost. Not only does their teddy-bear appearance belie great
strength, but as Alexander Jones realizes at the close of Earthman's
Burden (1957 [A62]), their love of imitation is more than a source of
hilarious antics: it is part of their adaptability, a "special talent
by which they may one day succeed us as the political leaders of the
galaxy." The Dilbians seem little more than primitive and simple-
minded giants, but as one of them shrewdly reminds the human protagonist at the end of Spacial Delivery (1961 [A113]), "Appearances . . .
are often deceiving." Significantly, the insight achieved by the human protagonist of the second novel in series, Spacepaw, into "the way
the Dilbians do things is that whatever is obvious is a smoke screen
for the real thing."

Contact with aliens demands that humans shed their illusions and
recognize the truth, for only thus can they learn about themselves.
Failure to do so leaves them impoverished spiritually, like the father
in "The Christmas Present" (1958 [A79]). Unaware that an alien creature has just saved his life at the cost of its own, he sees only its
potential danger to himself and his family. Yet dangerous potential
is only a threat to the ignorant. Failure to understand and make the
right decision would have left the young humans marooned on a distant
planet in Space Winners, just as it would have earned disgrace and
probably death for the humans on Dilbia. Behind their comical exter-
ior, the aliens in stories like "Zeepsday" (1956 [A58]), "Undiplomatic
Immunity" (1957 [A69]), "Fleegl of Fleegl" (1958 [A81]), and "The
Faithful Wilf" pose a serious threat if the human protagonists prove
unable to solve the problems the former create. The consequences of
failure are demonstrated in "Ricochet on Miza" and "An Honorable
Death" (1961 [A115]), where the humans who seek wealth and ease lose
their lives, and in Naked to the Stars, where, until he expiates his
sin, Cal loses his soul for his massacre in the Lehaunen village.
Nevertheless, the power and dignity that can destroy when offended
also reward with loving friendship and acclaim once they have been
recognized and understood. And the path to understanding, Dickson
affirms, is empathy, the ability to put oneself in another's place.
In so doing, one also gains a clearer view of oneself, and perceives
the reality behind the illusion.

By putting mankind in situations of stress, Dickson proves to
some that their sense of impotence is an illusion, that they possess
resources that will enable them to cope; to others he demonstrates
that their sense of power is misplaced. A desperate situation can be
retrieved through courage and tenacity; yet blind loyalty and inflex-
ibility can bring about disaster if one does not realize the implications of one's actions. Superior strength and aggression can be

overcome by keen wits; the gentle power of empathy wins over hearts that the mighty power of the sword can never pierce.

Thus may mankind confidently venture naked to the stars. Athwart this path stands the symbolic figure of the alien, humorous yet grimly serious, bright with promise yet ominously threatening, a creature that lies in the future yet reaches back into the depths of a mythic past, a figure whose paradoxical nature must be recognized and given its due if mankind is to advance. For it is the paradox that lies within mankind's own soul. Behind the illusion of what some critics have mistaken in Dickson's work for facile optimism lies the reality of a golden future that can only be achieved and maintained at great cost. But it is a glorious challenge he invites us all to gladly undertake.

1. On the appeal of Dickson's adult fiction to younger readers, see my article "Gordon R. Dickson: Science Fiction for Young Canadians" [D254].

2. Dickson generally dislikes collaborating, but has done so under "very special circumstances," as he explained in an informative interview with Clifford McMurray (1978 [C55]). Apart from Anderson, he has collaborated with Keith Laumer on Planet Run (1967 [A160]), Ben Bova on Gremlins, Go Home! (1974 [A195]), and Harry Harrison on Lifeboat (1975 [A200]).

3. A short extract from the former was published in 1980 (see entry A227).

4. This identification is developed at greater length in my article "Shai Dorsai!: A Study of the Hero Figure in Gordon R. Dickson's Dorsai!" (D240).

5. This strain has been compared by some critics to Van Vogt, an author for whom Dickson had an early love (see entries D6, D23).

Abbreviations

ASF   Astounding Science Fiction, subsequently Analog Science
            Fiction/Science Fact

BBIP   British Books in Print

FSF   Magazine of Fantasy and Science Fiction

KR   Kirkus Reviews

LJ   Library Journal

PW   Publishers Weekly

SFBC   Science Fiction Book Club

SFBRI Science Fiction Book Review Index

WIF   Worlds of If

Part A: Fiction

1942

A1 "MacGregor." Tycho [fanzine] 1, no. 1 (June):6-10.

A2 "If I Werewolf" (Part VII). [Minneapolis Fantasy Society, pseud.]. With Sam Russell. Spaceways [fanzine] 4, no. 7, pt. 7 (September):7-10, 12. [Note: Each episode of this "serial" was written by a different individual or group, in this case Dickson and Russell for the Minneapolis Fantasy Society, and it introduces various science fiction fans into the story. Each changes into some kind of creature: Dickson becomes a Jabberwock. See MFS Bulletin (fanzine) 1, no. 5 ([August?] 1942):4.]

A3 "Double Doublecross." Minnesota Technolog 22 (October):198-99, 222. [Note: First of a series of stories published by Dickson while an undergraduate at the University of Minnesota, in the Engineering Department's magazine. The series ended when Dickson was drafted into the army during the Second World War.]

A4 "Me & Rollo and Ju-Ju." Minnesota Technolog 23 (October):26.

1943

A5 "Pluggy Goes to Hell." Minnesota Technolog 23 (January):104, 112.

A6 "Mary Saves the Day." Minnesota Technolog 23 (February):130-31, 152.

1950

A7 "Trespass!" With Poul Anderson. Fantastic Story Quarterly 1 (Spring):131-41, 160. [Note: First story published in a professional magazine.]

Everett F. Bleiler and T. E. Dikty, eds. The Best Science
   Fiction Stories: 1951. New York: Frederick Fell.
Anon., ed. The Mindworm. London: Tandem, 1967 [paper].
   [Note: Reprints most, but not all, of the stories in the
   Bleiler and Dikty anthology; does not credit editors.]

1951

A8   "The Friendly Man." ASF 46 (February):114-25. [Note: First
      story solely by Dickson published in a professional maga-
      zine.]

      In Ancient, My Enemy, 1974 (A198).

A9   "Heroes Are Made." With Poul Anderson. Other Worlds Science
         Stories 3 (May):38-53. [Note: First of the Hoka series.]

         As "The Sheriff of Canyon Gulch." In Earthman's Burden,
            1957 (A62). [Note: All subsequent appearances use this
            title.]
         Robert Silverberg, ed. The Science Fiction Bestiary: Nine
            Stories of Science Fiction. New York and Camden, N.J.:
            Thomas Nelson, 1971.
         Andre Norton and Ernestine Donaldy, eds. Gates to Tomorrow:
            An Introduction to Science Fiction. New York: Atheneum,
            1973.
         Roger Elwood, ed. The Many Worlds of Poul Anderson. Radnor,
            Pa.: Chilton, 1974. Rpt. as The Book of Poul Anderson.
            New York: DAW, 1975 [paper].

A10   "The Error of Their Ways." ASF 47 (July):115-27.

A11   "The Monkey Wrench." ASF 47 (August):130-40.

         Brian W. Aldiss, ed. More Penguin Science Fiction.
            Harmondsworth, Middlesex: Penguin, 1963 [paper].
         Damon Knight, ed. The Metal Smile. New York: Belmont,
            1968 [paper].
         In Ancient, My Enemy, 1974 (A198).

A12   "Tommy Two-Gun." 10 Story Western Magazine 44 (August):42-48.
         [Note: The first of Dickson's two published western stories
         (see also entry A29). Unpublished western stories are
         listed in the inventory of Dickson manuscripts held in the
         special collections of the University of Minnesota libraries,
         hereafter cited as Dickson Papers (see Appendix A).]

A13   "The Star-Fool." Planet Stories 5 (September):50-56.

Part A: Fiction

A14   "Steel Brother." ASF 48 (February):103-24.

> Andre Norton, ed. Space Service. Cleveland and New York:
> World Publishing Co., 1953.
> In Danger--Human, 1970 (A172).

A15   "Ricochet on Miza." Planet Stories 5 (March):31-35.

> In Combat SF, 1975 (A203).

A16   "The Stranger." Imagination Stories of Science and Fantasy
> 3 (May):104-12.

A17   "Listen." FSF 3 (August):79-84. [Note: The first of many
> sales to FSF. In FSF 58 (March 1980):157, Dickson is listed
> among those writers who have had the largest number of sto-
> ries published in the magazine. His total of twenty-nine
> place him seventh, equal with Fritz Leiber.]

> Donald A. Wollheim, ed. Prize Science Fiction. New York:
> McBride, 1953. Rpt. as Prize Stories of Space and Time.
> London: Weidenfeld, Nicolson, 1953.
> In Mutants, 1970 (A173).
> In Love Not Human, 1981 (A230).

A18   "The Mousetrap." Galaxy 4 (September):117-31. [Note: First
> sale to Galaxy.]

> In The Star Road, 1973 (A192).

A19   "The Invaders." Space Stories 1 (October):72-100. [Note:
> Also entitled "Natural Enemy."]

> Helen Tono, ed. Science Fiction Yearbook, no. 2. New York:
> Popular Library, 1968 [paper].

A20   "Show Me the Way to Go Home." Startling Stories 28 (December):
> 83-90.

> Helen Tono, ed. Science Fiction Yearbook, no. 1. New York:
> Popular Library, 1967 [paper].

A21   "Time Grabber." Imagination Stories of Science and Fantasy 3
> (December):108-21. [Note: Also entitled "Intertime
> Incident."]

Part A: Fiction

1953

A22 "No Shield from the Dead." <u>WIF</u> 1 (January):111–15. [Note: First sale to <u>WIF</u>; also entitled "A Very Clever Game."]

A23 "The Bleak and Barren Land." <u>Space Stories</u> 1 (February):86–111.

    In <u>Ancient, My Enemy</u>, 1974 (A198).

A24 "Babes in the Wood." <u>Other Worlds Science Stories</u>, no. 29 (May):82–96.

A25 "The Three." <u>Startling Stories</u> 30 (May):123–30.

    Jim Hendryx, Jr., ed. <u>Treasury of Great Science Fiction Stories</u>, no. 1. New York: Popular Library, 1964 [paper].
    Francis J. McComas, ed. <u>Special Wonder: The Anthony Boucher Memorial Anthology of Fantasy and Science Fiction</u>. New York: Random House, 1970.

A26 "In Hoka Signo Vinces." With Poul Anderson. <u>Other Worlds</u>, no. 30 (June):70–87. [Note: Second of the Hoka series.]

    In <u>Earthman's Burden</u>, 1957 (A62).

A27 "Graveyard." <u>Future Science Fiction</u> 4 (July):10–24.

    In <u>Love Not Human</u>, 1981 (A230).

A28 "The Man the Worlds Rejected." <u>Planet Stories</u> 6 (July):14–35. [Note: Author's name erroneously reversed to Dickson Gordon.]

A29 "Practice Makes Perfect." <u>Texas Western</u> 2 (July):72–77. [Note: Second of Dickson's two published westerns (see also entry A12).]

A30 "The Breaking of Jerry McCloud." <u>Universe Science Fiction</u>, no. 2 (September):47–63.

    In <u>Love Not Human</u>, 1981 (A230).

A31 "Counter-Irritant." <u>Future Science Fiction</u> 4 (November):42–51.

A32 "The Adventure of the Misplaced Hound." With Poul Anderson. <u>Universe Science Fiction</u>, no. 3 (December):50–74. [Note: Third of the Hoka series.]

    In <u>Earthman's Burden</u>, 1957 (A62).
    Robert C. Peterson, ed. <u>The Science-Fictional Sherlock</u>

Holmes. Denver: Council of Four, 1960.

1954

A33 "The Rebels." Fantastic Story Magazine 6 (Winter):95-104.
[Note: This issue precedes Spring 1954, which is the first
of vol. 7, hence was published early in 1954. Copyright
date is 1953.]

A34 "Lulungomeena." Galaxy 7 (January):70-88. [Note: This story
introduces the Dorsai in the figure of the narrator. However, it is not part of the author's Childe Cycle, which
was conceived in 1960.]

Milton Lesser, ed. Looking Forward. New York: Beechurst
Press, 1953. [Note: Although this anthology acknowledges
that the story was copyrighted by Galaxy in 1953, the an-
thology appearance seems to have predated that in the
magazine.]
In Danger--Human, 1970 (A172).
Robert Silverberg, ed. Deep Space: Eight Stories of
Science Fiction. Nashville, Camden, N.J., and New York:
Thomas Nelson, 1973.

A35 "Black Charlie." Galaxy 8 (April):123-37. [Note: Basis of
later novel Alien Art (A189).]

H. L. Gold, ed. The Fifth Galaxy Reader. New York:
Doubleday, 1961.
Damon Knight, ed. One Hundred Years of Science Fiction.
New York: Simon & Schuster, 1968.
In Danger--Human, 1970 (A172).
Thomas F. Monteleone, ed. The Arts and Beyond: Visions
of Man's Aesthetic Future. Garden City, N.Y.: Doubleday,
1977.
In Love Not Human, 1981 (A230).

A36 "Miss Prinks." FSF 6 (June):22-32.

In Mutants, 1970 (A173).

A37 "Rescue." Future Science Fiction 5 (June):112-21.

A38 "Itco's Strong Right Arm." Cosmos Science Fiction and Fantasy
Magazine, no. 4 (July):33-51. [Note: First word of title
misspelled "Itko" in table of contents.]

A39 "Fellow of the Bees." Orbit Science Fiction 1 (July-August):
36-54.

Part A: Fiction

A40   "Carry Me Home." _WIF_ 4 (November):30-51.

A41   "The Queer Critter." Orbit Science Fiction 1 (November-
       December):17-19.

A42   "A Case History." _FSF_ 7 (December):63-67.

                            1955

A43   "Turnabout." _WIF_ 4 (January):86-103.

A44   "The Odd Ones." _WIF_ 4 (February):6-21.

       James L. Quinn and Eve Wulff, eds. The Second Worlds of If.
           Kingston, N.Y.: Quinn Publishing, 1958 [paper].
       In Ancient, My Enemy, 1974 (A198).

A45   "Yo Ho Hoka!" With Poul Anderson. _FSF_ 8 (March):95-118.
       [Note: Fourth of the Hoka series.]

       In Earthman's Burden, 1957 (A62).

A46   "James." _FSF_ 8 (May):49-53.

       In Danger--Human, 1970 (A172).

A47   "Moon, June, Spoon, Croon." Startling Stories 33 (Summer):
       27-30.

       In Love Not Human, 1981 (A230).

A48   "Perfectly Adjusted." Science Fiction Stories 6 (July):4-56.
       [Note: Later expanded into a novel as Delusion World (see
       entry A112).]

A49   "Our First Death." _FSF_ 9 (August):43-56.

       In Ancient, My Enemy, 1974 (A198).

A50   "The Tiddlywink Warriors." With Poul Anderson. _FSF_ 9
       (August):105-26. [Note: Fifth in the Hoka series.]

       In Earthman's Burden, 1957 (A62).

A51   "No More Barriers." Original Science Fiction Stories 6
       (September):4-79. [Note: Later expanded into a novel as
       Time to Teleport (A102).]

A52   "Joy in Mudville." With Poul Anderson. _FSF_ 9 (November):
       104-26. [Note: Sixth in the Hoka series; not collected in

Earthman's Burden.]

Terry Carr, ed. <u>The Infinite Arena: Seven Science Fiction Stories about Sports</u>. Nashville and New York: Thomas Nelson, 1977.

A53   "Of the People." <u>FSF</u> 9 (December):76-79.

    In <u>Mutants</u>, 1970 (A173).
    In <u>Gordon R. Dickson's SF Best</u>, 1978 (A216).
    John Robert Colombo, ed. <u>Other Canadas: An Anthology of Science Fiction and Fantasy</u>. Toronto, Halifax, Montreal, and Vancouver: McGraw-Hill Ryerson, 1979.

A54   "The Underground." <u>Imagination Stories of Science and Fantasy</u> 6 (December):74-89. [Note: Also entitled "The Little Captain."]

1956

A55   <u>Alien from Arcturus</u>. New York: Ace [paper]. [Note: Dickson's first novel, published as an Ace Double (D-139) with Nick Boddie Williams, <u>The Atom Curtain</u>. It introduces the delightful alien Peep, who reappears in <u>The Space Winners</u> (A154).]

    As <u>Arcturus Landing</u>. New York: Ace, 1978 [rev. text]; [paper]. [Note: The changes include naming the hero Malcolm Fletcher instead of Johnny Parent, though the publisher's blurb on the back cover continues to refer to him as Parent. Dickson uses Parent as the name of a hero of several short stories, beginning with "Rex and Mr. Rejilla," 1958 (A80), and he may have made the change to avoid confusion. Includes essay by Sandra Miesel, "About Gordon R. Dickson" (see entry D222).]

A56   <u>Mankind on the Run</u>. New York: Ace [paper]. [Note: Bound with Andre Norton, <u>The Crossroads of Time</u>, as an Ace Double (D-164).]

    As <u>On the Run</u>. New York: Ace, 1979 [paper].

A57   "Flat Tiger." <u>Galaxy</u> 11 (March):36-49. [Note: Also entitled "Final Contact."]

    In <u>Danger--Human</u>, 1970 (A172).
    <u>Argosy</u> 31 (October 1970):56-69.

A58   "Zeepsday." <u>FSF</u> 11 (November):83-98. [Note: Written in form of a court transcript.]

Part A: Fiction

In <u>Danger--Human</u>, 1970 (A172).

<u>Midwestern Advocate</u> 2 (January 1975):4, 10-15. [Note:
Published by the Student Bar Association of the
Midwestern School of Law at Hamline University, St.
Paul, Minnesota.]

In <u>In Iron Years</u>, 1980 (A229).

A59 "The Green Building." <u>Satellite Science Fiction</u> 1 (December):
123-28.

A60 "Strictly Confidential." <u>Fantastic Universe Science Fiction</u> 6
(December):112-28.

1957

A61 "Don Jones." With Poul Anderson. In <u>Earthman's Burden</u>. New
York: Gnome Press. [Note: Seventh in the Hoka series;
written specially for the collection.]

A62 <u>Earthman's Burden</u>. With Poul Anderson. Illustrations by Edd
Cartier. New York: Gnome Press. ["The Sheriff of Canyon
Gulch" ("Heroes Are Made"), 1951; "Don Jones," 1957; "In
Hoka Signo Vinces," 1953; "The Adventure of the Misplaced
Hound," 1953; "Yo Ho Hoka!" 1955; "The Tiddlywink Warriors,"
1955.]

New York: Camelot Books/Avon, 1970 [paper].
New York: Avon, 1979 [paper]. [Note: Includes the original illustrations by Edd Cartier.]

A63 "The Sheriff of Canyon Gulch." See "Heroes Are Made," 1951
(A9).

A64 "Rescue Mission." <u>FSF</u> 12 (January):78-94.

A65 "Friend for Life." <u>Venture Science Fiction</u> 1 (March):57-69.
[Note: Also entitled "Cry Bones."]

A66 "Tempus Non Fugit." <u>Original Science Fiction Stories</u> 7
(March):116-34.

A67 "Turn Again, Whittington." <u>Toronto Star Weekly Magazine</u>, 23
March, pp. 16-17. [Note: A romantic, non-science fiction
story.]

A68 "Act of Creation." <u>Satellite Science Fiction</u> 1 (April):93-102.
[Note: Second story to include the Dorsai (see also entry
A34); not part of the Childe Cycle, although it shows signs
of fuller development of political situation that finally
evolves.]

Part A: Fiction

In <u>Gordon R. Dickson's SF Best</u>, 1978 (A216).

A69 "Undiplomatic Immunity." With Poul Anderson. <u>FSF</u> 12 (May):
     79-101. [Note: Eighth in the Hoka series.]

A70 "Mx Knows Best." <u>Saturn Magazine of Fantasy and Science-
     Fiction</u> 1 (July):2-23. [Note: Also entitled "Cancel."]

A71 "Cloak and Stagger." <u>Future Science Fiction</u>, no. 34 (Fall):
     18-41.

A72 "St. Dragon and the George." <u>FSF</u> 13 (September):94-124.
     [Note: Later expanded into a novel as <u>The Dragon and the
     George</u> (A206).]

A73 "Full Pack (Hokas Wild)." With Poul Anderson. <u>FSF</u> 13
     (October):105-25. [Note: Ninth of the Hoka series.]

A74 "Robots Are Nice?" <u>Galaxy</u> 14 (October):108-21.

A75 "Fido." <u>FSF</u> 13 (November):85-99.

     In <u>Love Not Human</u>, 1981 (A230).

A76 "The General and the Axe." <u>Infinity Science Fiction</u> 3
     (November):4-33.

A77 "Danger--Human!" <u>ASF</u> 60 (December):64-80.

     In <u>Danger--Human</u>, 1970 (A172).
     In <u>Mutants</u>, 1970 (A173).
     Robert Silverberg, ed. <u>Strange Gifts: Eight Stories of
     Science Fiction</u>. Nashville and New York: Thomas Nelson,
     1975.

A78 "With Butter and Mustard." <u>FSF</u> 13 (December):78-89.

                              1958

A79 "The Christmas Present." <u>FSF</u> 13 (January):34-42.

     In <u>The Star Road</u>, 1973 (A192).
     Sylvia Engdahl and Rick Robertson, eds. <u>Universe Ahead:
     Stories of the Future</u>. New York: Atheneum, 1975.
     Terry Carr, ed. <u>To Follow a Star: Nine Science Fiction
     Stories about Christmas</u>. Nashville and New York:
     Thomas Nelson, 1977.
     In <u>Love Not Human</u>, 1981 (A230).

A80 "Rex and Mr. Rejilla." <u>Galaxy</u> 15 (January):70-87. [Note:

First of a lighthearted series of four tales involving Tom
and Lucy Parent (see also entries A132, A139, A147).]

A81 "Fleegl of Fleegl." Venture Science Fiction 2 (May):60-76.
[Note: Also entitled "Nobody's Mad at Fleegl."]

A82 "A Matter of Technique." FSF 14 (May):56-68.

A83 "The Question." ASF 61 (May):56-71.

A84 "Brother Charlie." FSF 15 (July):5-33.

   In Gordon R. Dickson's SF Best, 1978 (A216).

A85 "Last Voyage." Original Science Fiction Stories 9 (July):66-81.
[Note: Also entitled "Last Voyage of the Teakettle."]

A86 "The Girl Who Played Wolf." Fantastic 7 (August):6-23, 100.
[Note: First story published in the field of supernatural
horror; also entitled "The Were-Wolfhound."]

   Strange Fantasy, no. 10 (Fall 1969):4-22. [Note: Last
      word of title misspelled "Woolf" in table of contents.]

A87 "The Quarry." ASF 62 (September):50-56.

   In Danger--Human, 1970 (A172).

A88 "Gifts." ASF 62 (November):88-99.

   In In Iron Years, 1980 (A229).

                        1959

A89 "The Dreamsman." In Star Science Fiction, No. 6. Edited by
Frederick Pohl. New York: Ballantine, pp. 99-106 [paper].
[Note: Also entitled "Mr. Willer Does His Bit."]

   Judith Merril, ed. The 5th Annual of the Year's Best S-F.
      New York: Simon & Schuster, 1960.

A90 "By New Hearth Fires." ASF 62 (January):40-53.

   In Mutants, 1970 (A173).

A91 "The R of A." FSF 16 (January):119-30.

A92 "After the Funeral." Fantastic 8 (April):20-23.

A93 "The Amulet." FSF 16 (April):47-61.

Rod Serling, ed. Rod Serling's Triple W: Witches, Warlocks and Werewolves. New York: Bantam, 1963 [paper]. [Note: Dickson edited this anthology under the house pseudonym of Rod Serling (see also entry A138).]

Leo P. Kelley. The Supernatural in Fiction. New York: McGraw-Hill, 1973 [paper].

A94   "The Catch." ASF 63 (April):67-77.

In The Star Road, 1973 (A192).

A95   "The Man in the Mailbag." Galaxy 17 (April):160-90. [Note: Later expanded into a novel as Spacial Delivery, 1961 (A113). First of a humorous series set on the planet Dilbia (see also entries A167, A180).]

A96   "Dorsai!" ASF 63 (May):8-54; (June):78-133; (July):62-119. [Note: First part of Dickson's Childe Cycle; runner-up for the 1960 Hugo Award in the novel category.]

As The Genetic General. New York: Ace, 1960 [paper]. [Note: Bound with Time to Teleport (A102) as an Ace Double (D-449). This version was cut and retitled by Ace against Dickson's wishes.]
London: Digit, 1961 [paper]. [Note: First publication of a Dickson novel in Britain.]
New York: Ace [1967] [paper]. [Note: First separate book appearance in the U.S.]
As Dorsai! London: Sphere, 1975 [paper]. [Note: Despite the change in title, this is still the cut version found in The Genetic General.]
In Three to Dorsai! 1975. [Note: First book appearance of the uncut version with narrative links to Necromancer and Tactics of Mistake, two other novels in the Childe Cycle (see entries A128, A178, A202).]
As Dorsai! New York: DAW, 1976 [paper]. [Note: First appearance of the uncut version as a separate book.]
New York: Ace, 1980. With afterword by Sandra Miesel [paper].

A97   "E Gubling Dow." Satellite Science Fiction 3 (May):21-27.

A98   "Homecoming." WIF 9 (September):66-83.

In In Iron Years, 1980 (A229).

A99   "I've Been Trying to Tell You." Fantastic Universe Science Fact & Fiction 12 (November):19-27. [Note: Also entitled "Ragnarok."]

Part A: Fiction

1960

A100   <u>The Genetic General</u>. See entry A96.

A101   <u>Secret under the Sea</u>. New York: Holt, Rinehart & Winston.
Illustrated by Jo Ann Stover. [Note: First of the Robby
Hoenig series, written for juveniles; also entitled <u>The Sea
Walker</u> (see also entries A134, A141).]

       London: Hutchinson, 1962. [Note: Second publication of a
Dickson novel in Britain, and first in hardcover; retains
original illustrations.]
New York, London, and Richmond Hill, Ontario: Scholastic
Book Services, 1966 [paper]. [Note: Retains Stover's
illustrations, but reduces their number.]

A102   <u>Time to Teleport</u>. New York: Ace, 1960 [paper]. [Note: Bound
with <u>The Genetic General</u> (see entry A96) as an Ace Double
(D-449). Enlarged from "No More Barriers," 1955 (A51).]

A103   "The Game of Five." <u>FSF</u> 18 (April):103-30.

A104   "It Hardly Seems Fair." <u>Amazing Science Fiction</u> 34 (April):
88-99.

       <u>Great Science Fiction Magazine</u>, no. 7 (1967):71-82.
In <u>Love Not Human</u>, 1981 (A230).

A105   "The Summer Visitors." <u>Fantastic Science Fiction Stories</u> 9
(April):55-69.

       <u>Thrilling Science Fiction</u>, October 1973, pp. 68-81, 89.
[Note: No volume or issue number.]
In <u>Love Not Human</u>, 1981 (A230).

A106   "One on Trial." <u>FSF</u> 18 (May):48-56.

A107   "The Last Dream." <u>FSF</u> 18 (July):58-64.

A108   "The Case of the Clumsy Cadaver." [Will Folke, pseud.].
<u>Keyhole Mystery Magazine</u> 1 (August):44-59. [Note: First
of two detective stories sold by Dickson, this one under a
house pseudonym (see also entry A116).]

A109   "Button, Button." <u>FSF</u> 19 (September):52-64.

A110   "The Hours Are Good." <u>Galaxy</u> 19 (October):151-61.

       In <u>In Iron Years</u>, 1980 (A229).

A111   "The Seats of Hell." <u>Fantastic Stories of the Imagination</u> 9
          (October):6-47.

                                1961

A112   <u>Delusion World</u>. New York: Ace [paper]. [Note: Enlarged
          from the novelette "Perfectly Adjusted" (A48), and bound
          with <u>Spacial Delivery</u> (A113) as an Ace Double (F-119). In-
          cludes a very brief autobiographical foreword by Dickson.]

A113   <u>Spacial Delivery</u>. New York: Ace [paper]. [Note: Enlarged
          from the novelette "The Man in the Mailbag" (A95) and bound
          with <u>Delusion World</u> (A112) as an Ace Double (F-119). First
          novel in the Dilbian series (see also entries A167, A180).]

       New York: Ace, 1979 [paper]. [Note: First separate pub-
          lication.]

A114   "Rehabilitated." <u>FSF</u> 20 (January):56-68.

       In <u>Mutants</u>, 1970 (A173).

A115   "An Honorable Death." <u>Galaxy</u> 19 (February):118-38.

          In <u>Danger--Human</u>, 1970 (A172).
          Damon Knight, ed. <u>A Pocketful of Stars</u>. Garden City,
             N.Y.: Doubleday, 1971.
          Robert Silverberg, ed. <u>Alpha 6</u>. New York: Berkley, 1976
             [paper].
          Gardner R. Dozois and Jack M. Dann, eds. <u>Aliens!</u> New York:
             Pocket Books, 1980 [paper]. [Note: Illustrated by Jack
             Gaughan.]

A116   "Out of the Darkness." <u>Ellery Queen's Mystery Magazine</u> 37
          (February):58-66. [Note: Also entitled "Lighthouse Keeper."
          Dickson's second detective story, the only one published
          under his real name (see note to entry A108), and the only
          one published in Britain, where it appeared in the British
          edition of the magazine, no. 102 (July 1961):59-68.]

A117   "The Amateurs." <u>Science Fiction Adventures</u> 4 (March):86-102.
          [Note: Only story to appear exclusively in a British maga-
          zine.]

A118   "Minotaur." <u>WIF</u> 11 (March):52-67.

A119   "A Taste of Tenure." <u>WIF</u> 11 (July):83-106.

       In <u>In Iron Years</u>, 1980 (A229).

A120   "Whatever Gods There Be." <u>Amazing Stories: Fact and Science Fiction</u> 35 (July):100-15.

        <u>Most Thrilling Science Fiction Ever Told</u>, no. 5 (1967): 44-59.
        In <u>The Star Road</u>, 1973 (A192).

A121   "The Haunted Village." <u>FSF</u> 21 (August):113-29. [Note: Dickson's first supernatural horror story to appear in Britain, where it was reprinted in the British edition of the magazine, 3 (December 1961):2-19.]

        Robert P. Mills, ed. <u>The Best from Fantasy and Science Fiction: Eleventh Series</u>. Garden City, N.Y.: Doubleday, 1962.

A122   "Love Me True." <u>ASF</u> 68 (October):59-68.

        In <u>Ancient, My Enemy</u>, 1974 (A198).
        In <u>Love Not Human</u>, 1981 (A230).

A123   "Naked to the Stars." <u>FSF</u> 21 (October):88-128; (November): 85-129. [Note: Dickson's response to the militaristic tone of Heinlein's <u>Starship Troopers</u>. Dickson terms his work a "propagandistic novel."]

        <u>Naked to the Stars</u>. New York: Pyramid, 1961 [rev. text]; [paper].
        New York: Lancer, [1971]; [paper].
        New York: DAW, 1977 [paper].
        London: Sphere, 1978 [paper].

A124   <u>Naked to the Stars</u>. See entry A123.

A125   "Sleight of Wit." <u>ASF</u> 68 (December):137-51. [Note: First of a series of three humorous tales about Hank Shallo, world scout (see also entries A148, A150).]

        John W. Campbell, Jr., ed. <u>Analog 1</u>. Garden City, N.Y.: Doubleday, 1963.

1962

A126   "Idiot Solvant." <u>ASF</u> 68 (January):45-59.

        Groff Conklin, ed. <u>13 Above the Night</u>. New York: Dell, 1965 [paper].
        In <u>Mutants</u>, 1970 (A173).
        In <u>Gordon R. Dickson's SF Best</u>, 1978 (A216).

A127   "Napoleon's Skullcap." <u>FSF</u> 22 (May):31-47.

A128   <u>Necromancer</u>. Garden City, N.Y.: Doubleday, 1962. Reprint.
        Science Fiction Book Club. [Note: Second novel in the
        Childe Cycle. Events precede those in <u>Dorsai!</u> (see entry
        A96), but the themes develop from the earlier novel.]

        London: Mayflower, 1963 [paper]. [Note: First paperback
            edition.]
        As <u>No Room for Man</u>. New York: Macfadden-Bartell, 1963
            [paper]. [Note: Title changed by publisher without
            consent of author.]
        New York: Manor, 1972 [paper]. [Note: <u>No Room for Man</u>
            went through two printings as a Macfadden Book, the sec-
            ond in 1966. Manor was the new name for Macfadden-Bartell,
            and so this is the third printing of this edition by the
            same publisher. Manor also published a "second edition"
            in 1974.]
        As <u>Necromancer</u> in <u>Three to Dorsai!</u>, 1975. [Note: Hereafter,
            resumes original title.]
        New York: DAW, 1978 [paper]. [Note: First U.S. paperback
            appearance with original title.]
        London: Sphere, 1979 [paper].
        New York: Ace, 1981 [paper].

A129   "Three-Part Puzzle." <u>ASF</u> 69 (June):43-54.

        In <u>The Star Road</u>, 1973 (A192).

A130   "Salmanazer." <u>FSF</u> 23 (August):19-26.

A131   "And Then There Was Peace." <u>WIF</u> 12 (September):46-48.

        In <u>Danger--Human</u>, 1970 (A172).

A132   "Who Dares a Bulbur Eat?" <u>Galaxy</u> 21 (October):174-90. [Note:
        Also entitled "Greater Love Hath." Second in series of four
        tales about Tom and Lucy Parent (see entries A80, A139,
        A147).]

A133   "Roofs of Silver." <u>FSF</u> 23 (December):93-116.

        In <u>Mutants</u>, 1970 (A173).

                            1963

A134   <u>Secret under Antarctica</u>. Illustrated by Charles Geer. New
        York, Chicago, and San Francisco: Holt, Rinehart & Winston.
        [Note: Second of the Robby Hoenig series for juveniles (see
        entries A101, A141).]

                            15

A135   "The Hard Way." <u>ASF</u> 70 (January):6-41. [Note: Also entitled
        "Watch that Worm." Later expanded into a novel as <u>The Alien</u>
        <u>Way</u> (A146).]

A136   "Hilifter." <u>ASF</u> 70 (February):58-75. [Note: Sequel <u>None but</u>
        <u>Man</u> (see entry A165).]

          John W. Campbell, Jr., ed. <u>Analog 3</u>. Garden City, N.Y.:
              Doubleday, 1965. [Note: Rpt. as <u>A World by the Tale</u>.
              New York: Curtis, 1965 (paper).]
          Thomas E. Sanders, ed. <u>Speculations: An Introduction to</u>
              <u>Literature through Fantasy and Science Fiction</u>. New
              York and Beverly Hills: Glencoe Press; Toronto: Collier
              Macmillan Canada, 1973 [paper].
          In <u>The Star Road</u>, 1973 (A192).
          In <u>Gordon R. Dickson's SF Best</u>, 1978 (A216).

A137   "Home from the Shore." <u>Galaxy</u> 21 (February):8-46. [Note:
        Also entitled "Hey Johnny." Sequel to <u>The Space Swimmers</u>
        (A162).]

          Judith Merril, ed. <u>The 8th Annual of the Year's Best S-F</u>.
              New York: Simon & Schuster, 1963.
          In <u>Mutants</u>, 1970 (A173).
          Charles N. Brown, ed. <u>Far Travellers: Three Science</u>
              <u>Fiction Novellas</u>. London and Westport, Conn.: Mews,
              1976 [paper].
          <u>Home from the Shore</u>. Illustrated by James R. Odbert. After-
              word by Sandra Miesel. New York: Sunridge Press, 1978
              [paper; trade paperback format]. [Note: Revised and ex-
              panded text; foreword by author (see entry C53).]
          New York: Ace, 1979 [paper; mass market format of preced-
              ing].

A138   <u>Rod Serling's Triple W: Witches, Warlocks and Werewolves</u>.
        [Rod Serling, pseud.]; [anthology]. New York: Bantam
        [paper]. [Note: First of two anthologies edited by Dickson
        under this house pseudonym. Includes "The Amulet" (A93; see
        also entry A161).]

A139   "The Faithful Wilf." <u>Galaxy</u> 21 (June):140-57. [Note: Table
        of contents omits first word of title. Third of four stories
        about Tom and Lucy Parent (see also entries A80, A132, A147).]

A140   <u>No Room for Man</u>. See <u>Necromancer</u>, 1962 (A128).

                                1964

A141   <u>Secret under the Caribbean</u>. New York, Chicago, and San
        Francisco: Holt, Rinehart & Winston. [Note: Third and

                                  16

last of the Robby Hoenig series for juveniles (see also
A101, A134).]

A142   "Dolphin's Way." ASF 73 (June):28-36.

  In Danger--Human, 1970 (A172).
  In Gordon R. Dickson's SF Best, 1978 (A216).
  Rod Serling, ed. Rod Serling's Other Worlds. Toronto, New
    York, and London: Bantam, 1978 [paper].
  James Gunn, ed. The Road to Science Fiction #3: From
    Heinlein to Here. New York and Scarborough, Ontario:
    New American Library, Mentor; London: New English
    Library, 1979 [paper].

A143   "The Man from Earth." Galaxy 22 (June):67-81.

  In Danger--Human, 1970 (A172).

A144   "On Messenger Mountain." Worlds of Tomorrow 2 (June):7-49.

  In The Star Road, 1973 (A192).

A145   "Soldier, Ask Not." Galaxy 23 (October):7-63. [Note: Part
    of the Childe Cycle and winner of the 1965 Hugo Award for
    best short story. This is one-third of the novel published
    under the same title (see entry A163).]

  Isaac Asimov, ed. The Hugo Winners, vol. 2. Garden City,
    N.Y.: Doubleday, 1971.

                              1965

A146   The Alien Way. New York, Toronto, and London: Bantam [paper].
    [Note: Issued in North America in February, in Britain in
    April. The opening section is based on "The Hard Way"
    (A135).]

  London: Corgi, 1973 [paper].
  New York, Toronto, and London: Bantam, 1973 [paper].
    [Note: Described as a "new edition," but the author has
    not copyrighted any new material, and so it would appear
    to be a reprint as far as content is concerned.]
  London: Sphere, 1979 [paper].

A147   "A Wobble in Wockii Futures." Galaxy 23 (April):68-94. [Note:
    Fourth and last of the series about Tom and Lucy Parent (see
    also entries A80, A132, A139).]

A148   "Soupstone." ASF 75 (July):81-103. [Note: Second of three
    stories about Hank Shallo (see also entries A125, A150).]

Part A: Fiction

A149   "The Immortal." FSF 29 (August):96-128.

  In Mutants, 1970 (A173).

A150   "Catch a Tartar." Worlds of Tomorrow 3 (September):5-28.
  [Note: Last of three stories about Hank Shallo (see also
  entries A125, A148).]

A151   "Computers Don't Argue." ASF 76 (September):84-94. [Note:
  Dickson's most anthologized story. Nominated for a Nebula
  Award in 1965 in the short story category. Also adapted as
  a play (see entry B6).]

   Damon Knight, ed. Nebula Award Stories 1965. Garden City,
    N.Y.: Doubleday, 1966.
   John W. Campbell, Jr., ed. Analog 5. Garden City, N.Y.:
    Doubleday, 1967.
   Harry Harrison and Brian W. Aldiss, eds. The Astounding-
    Analog Reader, vol. 2. Garden City, N.Y.: Doubleday,
    1973.
   Robert Hoskins, ed. Wondermakers 2. Greenwich, Conn.:
    Fawcett, 1974 [paper].
   Computer Decisions 6 (September 1974):17-20 [Note: Trade
    magazine.]
   Daniel Roselle, ed. Transformations II: Understanding
    American History through Science Fiction. Greenwich,
    Conn.: Fawcett, 1974 [paper].
   Bernard Hollister, ed. You and Science Fiction: A
    Humanistic Approach to Tomorrow. Skokie, Ill.: National
    Textbook Co., 1976 [paper].
   Creative Computing 2 (March-April 1976):11-15.
   D. Van Tassel, ed. Computers, Computers, Computers: In
    Fiction and Verse. Nashville and New York: Thomas
    Nelson, 1977.
   Brian W. Aldiss and Harry Harrison, eds. Decade: The 1960s.
    London: Macmillan, 1977.
   Patricia Warrick, Martin Harry Greenberg, and Joseph Olander,
    eds. Science Fiction: Contemporary Mythology: The
    SFWA-SFRA Anthology. New York, Hagerstown, San Francisco,
    and London: Harper & Row, 1978.
   Isaac Asimov, Martin H. Greenberg, and Joseph Olander, eds.
    Space Mail. New York: Fawcett, 1980 [paper].
   Stanley Schmidt, ed. The Analog Anthology #1. New York:
    Davis Publications, 1980 [paper].

A152   Mission to Universe. New York: Berkley [paper].

  New York: Ballantine, 1977 [rev. text]; [paper]. [Note:
   Ending changed.]
  London: Sphere, 1978 [paper].

Part A: Fiction

A153   "An Ounce of Emotion." <u>WIF</u> 15 (October):92-111.

A154   <u>Space Winners</u>. New York, Chicago, and San Francisco: Holt, Rinehart & Winston. [Note: First novel written for adolescents rather than juveniles (see entries A101, A134, A141). Reintroduces the alien Peep, who first appeared in <u>Alien from Arcturus</u> (A55).]

   London: Faber & Faber, 1967.

A155   "Tiger Green." <u>WIF</u> 15 (November):5-23. [Note: Also entitled "Communications."]

   In <u>Ancient, My Enemy</u>, 1974 (A198).
   In <u>Gordon R. Dickson's SF Best</u>, 1978 (A216).

A156   "Breakthrough Gang." <u>FSF</u> 29 (December):5-20.

A157   "Warrior." <u>ASF</u> 76 (December):54-73. [Note: An illumination of the Childe Cycle. Also entitled "The Duty of Ian Graeme."]

   Judith Merril, ed. <u>11th Annual Edition: The Year's Best S-F</u>. New York: Delacorte Press, 1966.
   In <u>Mutants</u>, 1970 (A173).
   Harry Harrison, ed. <u>SF: Authors' Choice 4</u>. New York: Putnam, 1974.
   Donald A. Wollheim, ed. <u>The DAW Science Fiction Reader</u>. New York: DAW, 1976 [paper].
   In <u>Lost Dorsai</u>, 1980 (A228).

1966

A158   "Call Him Lord." <u>ASF</u> 77 (May):31-49. [Note: Winner of the Nebula Award in 1966 in the novelette category; nominated for a Hugo in the same category in 1967.]

   Brian W. Aldiss and Harry Harrison, eds. <u>Nebula Award Stories Two</u>. Garden City, N.Y.: Doubleday, 1967.
   John W. Campbell, Jr., ed. <u>Analog 6</u>. Garden City, N.Y.: Doubleday, 1968.
   In <u>Danger--Human</u>, 1970 (A172).
   Martin Harry Greenberg and Patricia S. Warrick, eds. <u>Political Science Fiction: An Introductory Reader</u>. Englewood Cliffs, N.J.: Prentice-Hall, 1974. [Note: Issued simultaneously in both hardcover and paperback.]
   Lee Harding, ed. <u>Beyond Tomorrow: An Anthology of Modern Science Fiction</u>. Melbourne: Wren Publishing, 1976 [paper].
   <u>Call Him Lord</u>. Carson, Calif.: Educational Insights,

1977. [Note: Illustrated comic version, 4 pages long, with educational questions at the end.]
In Gordon R. Dickson's SF Best, 1978 (A216).
Élan Vital: Journal of Creative Adventure 1, no. 3 [June 1979]:178-87.

A159   "In the Bone." WIF 16 (October):140-59.

In Ancient, My Enemy, 1974 (A198).
In Gordon R. Dickson's SF Best, 1978 (A216).

1967

A160   Planet Run. With Keith Laumer. Garden City, N.Y.: Doubleday. [Note: Dickson's first collaboration on a full-length novel.]

New York: Berkley, 1968 [paper].
London: Robert Hale, 1977.

A161   Rod Serling's Devils and Demons. [Rod Serling, pseud.]; [anthology]. Toronto, New York, and London: Bantam [paper]. [Note: Second of two anthologies edited by Dickson under this house pseudonym (see also entry A138).]

A162   The Space Swimmers. New York: Berkley [paper]. [Note: Sequel to "Home from the Shore" (A137).]

London: Sidgwick & Jackson, 1970.
Science Fiction Special 1. London: Sidgwick & Jackson, 1970.
New York: Ace, 1979 [paper]. [Note: Illustrated by Steve Fabian.]

A163   Soldier, Ask Not. New York: Dell [paper]. [Note: One-third of this novel, under the same title, was published in Galaxy in 1964 (see entry A145). Third novel of the Childe Cycle.]

London: Sphere, 1975 [paper].
New York: DAW, 1975 [paper].
New York: Ace, 1980 [paper].

1968

A164   "Building on the Line." Galaxy 27 (November):84-121.

In The Star Road, 1973 (A192).

Part A: Fiction

1969

A165   None but Man. Garden City, N.Y.: Doubleday. [Note: Also
          entitled "Spacelifter's War." Sequel to "Hilifter" (A136).]

          London: Macdonald Science Fiction, 1969.
          New York: Pyramid, 1971 [paper].
          New York: DAW, 1977 [paper].

A166   "Wolfling." ASF 82 (January):8-43; (February):100-54; 83
          (March):118-66.

          Wolfling. New York: Dell, 1969 [paper].

A167   Spacepaw. New York: Putnam. [Note: Second novel in the
          Dilbian series (see also entries A95, A113, A180).]

          New York: Berkley, 1969 [paper].

A168   Wolfling. See entry A166.

A169   "Hour of the Horde." Venture Science Fiction 3 (May):4-91.

          Hour of the Horde. New York: Putnam, 1970.
          New York: Berkley, 1971 [paper].
          New York: DAW, 1978 [paper].

A170   "Jackal's Meal." ASF 83 (June):140-59.

          In The Star Road, 1973 (A192).

A171   "Ancient, My Enemy." WIF 19 (December):4-39.

          In Ancient, My Enemy, 1974 (A198).

1970

A172   Danger--Human. Garden City, N.Y.: Doubleday. ["Danger--
          Human!" 1957; "Dolphin's Way," 1964; "And Then There Was
          Peace," 1962; "The Man from Earth," 1964; "Black Charlie,"
          1954; "Zeepsday," 1956; "Lulungomeena," 1954; "An Honorable
          Death," 1961; "Flat Tiger," 1956; "James," 1955; "The
          Quarry," 1958; "Call Him Lord," 1966; "Steel Brother,"
          1952.]

          As The Book of Gordon Dickson. New York: DAW, 1973 [paper].

A173   Mutants: A Science Fiction Adventure. New York: Macmillan.
          ["Warrior," 1965; "Of the People," 1955; "Danger--Human!"
          1957; "Rehabilitated," 1961; "Listen," 1952; "Roofs of

Silver," 1962; "By New Hearth Fires," 1959; "Idiot Solvant,"
1962; "The Immortal," 1965; "Miss Prinks," 1954; "Home from
the Shore," 1963.] [Note: Introduction by author provides
a thematic frame.]

New York: Collier, 1973 [paper].

A174 "Operation P-Button." In Infinity One, a Magazine of
Speculative Fiction in Book Form. Edited by Robert Hoskins.
New York: Lancer, pp. 133-34 [paper]. [Note: Story not
listed in table of contents.]

A175 "Walker between the Planes." Worlds of Fantasy 1 (February):
4-22, 97-130.

As "Maverick." In Keith Laumer, ed. Five Fates. Garden
City, N.Y.: Doubleday. [Note: Textual revisions to
integrate story into anthology framework involve change
of hero's name, modification of introductory and con-
cluding sections, and some stylistic adjustments.]

A176 "Maverick." See "Walker between the Planes," 1970 (A175).

A177 Hour of the Horde. See entry A169.

A178 "The Tactics of Mistake." ASF 86 (October):8-71; (November):
108-65; (December):118-63; (January 1971):88-137. [Note:
Nominated for a Nebula award, 1971, first ballot only.
Fourth novel in the Childe Cycle.]

The Tactics of Mistake. Garden City, N.Y.: Doubleday, 1971.
As Tactics of Mistake. New York: DAW, [1972]; [paper].
[Note: First printing lacks publication date; later
printings are dated.]
London: Sphere, 1975 [paper].
In Three to Dorsai! 1975 (A205).

A179 "Jean Duprès." In Nova 1. Edited by Harry Harrison. New
York: Delacorte Press, pp. 125-68. [Note: Nominated for
a Nebula award in the novelette category in 1970, first ballot only. Nominated for a Hugo award in the short story
category in 1971; placed third.]

Isaac Asimov, Charles G. Waugh, and Martin Harry Greenberg,
eds. The Seven Cardinal Virtues of Science Fiction. New
York: Fawcett, 1981 [paper].

1971

A180 "The Law-Twister Shorty." In The Many Worlds of Science

Fiction. Edited by Ben Bova. New York: Dutton, pp. 50-105. [Note: Last of the Dilbian series (see also entries A95, A113, A167).]

A181 The Tactics of Mistake. See entry A178.

A182 "The Outposter." ASF 87 (May):8-50; (June):122-68; (July): 102-47.

   The Outposter. Philadelphia and New York: Lippincott, 1972 [rev. text].
  London: Robert Hale, 1973.
  New York: Manor, 1973 [paper].
  London: Sphere, 1975 [paper].

A183 Sleepwalker's World. Philadelphia and New York: Lippincott.

   New York: DAW, 1972 [paper].
  London: Robert Hale, 1973.

1972

A184 The Outposter. See entry A182.

A185 "Things Which Are Caesar's." In The Day the Sun Stood Still: Three Original Novellas of Science Fiction. [Edited by Robert Silverberg.] Nashville and New York: Thomas Nelson, pp. 125-209. [Note: Nominated for a Nebula award in 1972, first ballot only.]

   In In Iron Years, 1980 (A229).

A186 "Powerway Emergency." Dimensions 1 (Spring):16-21. [Note: Trade magazine, published quarterly by Northern States Power Co.]

A187 "The Pritcher Mass." ASF 89 (August):8-60; 90 (September): 110-47; 90 (October):108-57. [Note: Nominated for a Nebula award in 1972, first ballot only.]

   The Pritcher Mass. Garden City, N.Y.: Doubleday, 1972.
  New York: DAW, 1973 [paper].

A188 The Pritcher Mass. See entry A187.

1973

A189 Alien Art. New York: Dutton. [Note: Originally intended as an expansion of "Black Charlie" (A35), but original story substantially revised.]

    London: Robert Hale, 1974.
New York: Ace, 1978 [paper]. [Note: Includes essay by
    Sandra Miesel, "About Gordon R. Dickson" (see entry
    D222).]

A190   "Brothers." In <u>Astounding: John W. Campbell Memorial
Anthology</u>. Edited by Harry Harrison. New York: Random
House, pp. 139-82. [Note: An Illumination of the Childe
Cycle.]

    In <u>The Spirit of Dorsai</u>, 1979 (A223).

A191   <u>The R-Master</u>. Philadelphia and New York: Lippincott. Reprint.
Science Fiction Book Club.

    New York: DAW, 1975 [paper].
London: Robert Hale, 1975.

A192   <u>The Star Road</u>. Garden City, N.Y.: Doubleday. Rpt. Science
Fiction Book Club. ["Whatever Gods There Be," 1961;
"Hilifter," 1963; "Building on the Line," 1968; "The
Christmas Present," 1958; "The Three-Part Puzzle," 1962;
"On Messenger Mountain," 1964; "The Catch," 1959; "Jackal's
Meal," 1969; "The Mousetrap," 1952.]

    New York: DAW, 1974 [paper].
London: Robert Hale, 1975.

A193   <u>The Book of Gordon R. Dickson</u>. See <u>Danger--Human</u>, 1970 (A172).

A194   "The Far Call." <u>ASF</u> 91 (August):10-51; 92 (September):94-144;
92 (October):110-59. [Note: Also entitled "Capsule" (see
also entry C47).]

    <u>The Far Call</u>. New York: Dial Press/James Wade, 1978 [rev.
    text]. Rpt. Science Fiction Book Club.
London: Sidgwick & Jackson, 1978.
New York: Dell, 1978 [paper].
London: Futura Publications, 1978 [paper].

1974

A195   <u>Gremlins, Go Home!</u> With Ben Bova. New York: St. Martin's
Press. [Note: Also entitled <u>Goblin Passage</u>. Dickson's
fourth novel for juveniles (see also entries A101, A134,
A141).]

    *London: St. James Press, 1976. [Source: <u>BBIP</u>.]

A196   "Enter a Pilgrim." <u>ASF</u> 93 (August):14-31. [Note: First of
        an ongoing series, destined to develop into a novel. The
        central character is Shane Everts. See also "The Cloak and
        the Staff" (A226).]

        Lester del Rey, ed. <u>Best Science Fiction Stories of the</u>
            <u>Year, Fourth Annual Collection</u>. New York: Dutton, 1975.

A197   "Twig." In <u>Stellar 1</u>. Edited by Judy-Lynn del Rey. New York:
        Ballantine, pp. 180-215 [paper].

        Donald A. Wollheim, ed. <u>The 1975 Annual World's Best SF</u>.
            New York: DAW, 1975 [paper]. [Note: Issued later in
            hardcover by the Science Fiction Book Club.]

A198   <u>Ancient, My Enemy</u>. Garden City, N.Y.: Doubleday. Rpt.
        Science Fiction Book Club. ["Ancient, My Enemy," 1969;
        "The Odd Ones," 1955; "The Monkey Wrench," 1951; "Tiger
        Green," 1965; "The Friendly Man," 1951; "Love Me True,"
        1961; "Our First Death," 1955; "In the Bone," 1966; "The
        Bleak and Barren Land," 1952.]

        New York: DAW, 1976 [paper].
        London: Sphere, 1978 [paper].

A199   "In Iron Years." <u>FSF</u> 47 (October):151-74.

        In <u>In Iron Years</u>, 1980 (A229).

                        1975

A200   "The Lifeboat." With Harry Harrison. <u>ASF</u> 95 (February):12-57;
        (March):122-67; (April):102-51. [Note: Nominated for a
        Nebula award in 1975, first ballot only. See Dickson's
        comments upon collaboration in entry C54).]

        As <u>The Lifeship</u>. New York, Hagerstown, San Francisco, and
            London: Harper & Row, 1976.
        New York: Pocket Books, 1977 [paper].
        As <u>Lifeboat</u>. London: Futura Publications, 1977 [paper].
        London: Dobson, 1978.

A201   <u>Star Prince Charlie</u>. With Poul Anderson. New York: Putnam.
        [Note: First full-length novel in the Hoka series. Written
        primarily for adolescents. Also entitled <u>A King for Talyina</u>.]

        New York: Berkley, 1977 [paper]. [Note: Text copy edited.]

A202   <u>Dorsai!</u> See entry A96.

A203   Combat SF [anthology]. Garden City, N.Y.: Doubleday. [Note: First anthology edited by Dickson under his own name.]

A204   "Pro." ASF 95 (September):8–58. [Note: Also entitled "Conversion Factor," "Shortcut," "Equal or Opposite." Nominated for a Nebula award in the novella category in 1975, first ballot only.]

        Pro. Illustrated by James Odbert. New York: Ace, 1978 [rev. text]; [paper]. [Note: Changes primarily involve expansion to greater length and alterations to both beginning and end.]

A205   Three to Dorsai! Three Novels from the Childe Cycle: Necromancer, Tactics of Mistake, Dorsai! Garden City, N.Y.: Nelson Doubleday. [Necromancer, 1962; The Tactics of Mistake, 1970; Dorsai!, 1959.] [Note: Issued by the Science Fiction Book Club. The three novels make up a "substory" of the Childe Cycle, as is explained in the author's introduction (see entry C36). Links reinforced by a fictional frame. First appearance in book form of the uncut version of Dorsai! (see entries A96, A128, A178).]

1976

A206   The Dragon and the George. Garden City, N.Y.: Nelson Doubleday. [Note: Issued by the Science Fiction Book Club. Developed from "St. Dragon and the George" (A72). Nominated for a Nebula award in 1976, first ballot only. Winner of the 1976 British Fantasy Award of the British Fantasy Society.]

        New York: Ballantine, 1976 [paper].

A207   The Lifeship. See entry A200.

A208   "The Mortal and the Monster." In Stellar Short Novels. Edited by Judy-Lynn del Rey. New York: Ballantine, pp. 1–63 [paper]. [Note: Nominated for a Nebula award in novella category in 1976, first ballot only. Also entitled "The Youngest."]

        As "The Monster and the Maiden." In Love Not Human, 1981 (A230).

1977

A209   Lifeboat. See entry A200.

A210   "Time Storm." Isaac Asimov's Science Fiction Magazine 1
        (Spring):156-91. [Note: Excerpt from Time Storm (A213).
        Winner of Jupiter Award from Instructors of Science Fiction
        in Higher Education, in novelette category.]

A211   "Across the River." Isaac Asimov's Science Fiction Magazine 1
        (Summer):150-88. [Note: Second excerpt from Time Storm
        (A213), continuing from where "Time Storm" (A210) left off.]

A212   "Monad Gestalt." Cosmos: Science Fiction and Fantasy Magazine
        1 (July):47-67. [Note: Third excerpt from Time Storm
        (A213), continuing from where "Across the River" (A211)
        left off.]

A213   Time Storm. New York: St. Martin's Press. Rpt. Science
        Fiction Book Club. [Note: First part of novel appeared in
        three excerpts (see entries A210, A211, A212). Also entitled
        Time Trilogy: World of Mad Clocks; Half Past Eternity; Three
        Steps in Time. Nominated for 1977 Hugo Award in novel cate-
        gory.]

        London: Sphere, 1978 [paper].
        Toronto, New York, and London: Bantam, 1979 [paper].

                            1978

A214   The Far Call. See entry A194.

A215   Nebula Winners Twelve [anthology]. New York, Hagerstown, San
        Francisco, and London: Harper & Row. [Note: Published in
        Britain as Nebula Award Stories 12.]

        New York, Toronto, and London: Bantam, 1979 [paper].

A216   Gordon R. Dickson's SF Best. Edited by James R. Frenkel.
        Introduction and headnotes by Spider Robinson. New York:
        Dell [paper]. ["Hilifter," 1963; "Brother Charlie," 1958;
        "Act of Creation," 1957; "Idiot Solvant," 1961; "Call Him
        Lord," 1962; "Tiger Green," 1965; "Of the People," 1955;
        "Dolphin's Way," 1964; "In the Bone," 1966.]

A217   Home from the Shore. See entry A137.

A218   Arcturus Landing. See Alien from Arcturus, 1956 (A55).

A219   Pro. See entry A204.

Part A: Fiction

1979

A220 Masters of Everon. Garden City, N.Y.: Nelson Doubleday.
      [Note: Issued by Science Fiction Book Club. Also entitled
      Ecolog Mission.]

      New York: Ace, 1980 [paper].

A221 "Thank You, Beep . . . !" Hewlett-Packard Personal Calculator
      Digest 5:2-3, 28-29. [Note: Trade magazine. Story largely
      a vehicle to demonstrate the potential of computers in busi-
      ness.]

      Telecourier: A News Magazine for the RCC Industry 2
      (April 1979):12-13, 26, 28.

A222 "Amanda Morgan." In The Spirit of Dorsai. New York: Ace,
      pp. 11-168. [Note: An Illumination of the Childe Cycle.]

A223 The Spirit of Dorsai. Illustrated by Fernando Fernandez.
      New York: Ace [trade paperback format]. ["Amanda Morgan,"
      1979; "Brothers," 1973.] [Note: The two stories are set
      in a narrative frame.]

      New York: Ace, 1980 [paper]. [Note: Mass-market paperback,
      identical to trade version, but smaller format.]

A224 On the Run. See Mankind on the Run, 1956 (A56).

1980

A225 "Lost Dorsai." Destinies 2 (February-March):26-115. [Note:
      An Illumination of the Childe Cycle, here published in a
      cut version. Winner of the Hugo Award in the novella cate-
      gory.]

      In Lost Dorsai, 1980 [rev. text].

A226 "The Cloak and the Staff." ASF 100 (August):10-38. [Note:
      Second of an ongoing series, destined to be developed into
      a novel. The central character is Shane Everts. See also
      "Enter a Pilgrim" (A196). Winner of the Hugo Award in
      novellette category.]

A227 "The Final Encyclopedia: An Excerpt." In Lost Dorsai. New
      York: Ace, pp. 268-87. [Note: Excerpt from forthcoming
      fifth novel of the Childe Cycle.]

A228 Lost Dorsai. Illustrated by Fernando Fernandez. New York:
      Ace [trade paperback format]. ["Lost Dorsai," 1980;

"Warrior," 1965; Sandra Miesel, "The Plume and the Sword,"
1980 (see entry D249); "The Final Encyclopedia: An Excerpt,"
1980.]

A229   In Iron Years. Garden City, N.Y.: Doubleday. ["In Iron
        Years," 1974; "Homecoming," 1959; "A Taste of Tenure," 1961;
        "The Hours Are Good," 1960; "Gifts," 1958; "Zeepsday," 1956;
        "Things Which Are Caesar's," 1972.]

                              1981

A230   Love Not Human. New York: Ace [paper]. ["Black Charlie,"
        1954; "Moon, June, Spoon, Croon," 1955; "The Summer
        Visitors," 1960; "Listen," 1952; "Graveyard," 1953; "Fido,"
        1957; "The Breaking of Jerry McCloud," 1953; "Love Me True,"
        1961; "The Christmas Present," 1958; "It Hardly Seems Fair,"
        1960; "The Monster and the Maiden," 1976.] [Note: "The
        Monster and the Maiden" originally published as "The Mortal
        and the Monster" (A208).]

A231   "The Monster and the Maiden." See "The Mortal and the
        Monster," 1976 (A208).

Part B: Miscellaneous Media

*B1   "Lulungomeena." Radio Broadcast on NBC "X Minus One" program.
        [Source: Dickson, who records sale of radio rights in July.
        Adapted from original story (see entry A34).]

*B2   "Speak No More." Radio playscript for "Exploring Tomorrow"
        series.
        [Source: Dickson, who records sale on 3 February. Collected
        in Dickson Papers (see Appendix A).]

*B3   "The Great Gold Bear." Radio playscript for "Exploring
        Tomorrow" series.
        [Source: Dickson, who records sale on 10 March. Collected
        in Dickson Papers (see Appendix A).]

*B4   "Then Look behind You." Radio playscript for "Exploring
        Tomorrow" series.
        [Source: Dickson, who records sale on 6 April. Collected
        in Dickson Papers (see Appendix A).]

*B5   "The Gift." Radio playscript for "Exploring Tomorrow" series.
        [Source: Dickson, who records sale on 18 April. Collected
        in Dickson Papers (see Appendix A).]

*B6   "Noggo." Radio playscript for "Exploring Tomorrow" series.
        [Source: Dickson, who records sale on 18 April. Collected
        in Dickson Papers (see Appendix A).]

*B7   "Out of All Possible Times." Radio playscript for "Exploring
        Tomorrow" series.
        [Source: Dickson, who records sale on 1 May. Collected in
        Dickson Papers (see Appendix A).]

*B8   "The Decision." Radio playscript for "Exploring Tomorrow"
        series.

Part B: Miscellaneous Media

[Source: Dickson, who records sale on 31 May. Collected in Dickson Papers (see Appendix A).]

*B9 "The Seal." Radio playscript for "Exploring Tomorrow" series. [Source: Dickson, who records sale on 6 June with comment "Canadian Pacific Coast," presumably a reference to the setting. Two more radio playscripts, "The Greater Devil" and "Don't Call Me Joe," are listed as returned because "Mutual cancelled all dramatic shows." "The Seal" and "Don't Call Me Joe" are both collected in Dickson Papers (see Appendix A).]

1959

B10 "Guided Tour" [poem]. FSF 17 (October):59.

1961

B11 "Ballad of the Shoshonu" [song, both words and music]. In The 6th Annual of the Year's Best S-F. Edited by Judith Merril. New York: Simon & Schuster.

1964

B12 "Battle Hymn of the Friendly Soldiers" [song, no music]. Galaxy 23 (October):18. [Note: Part of "Soldier, Ask Not" (see entries A145, A163).]

   The NESFA Hymnal. Cambridge, Mass.: NESFA, n.d. [Note: Appears independent of "Soldier, Ask Not" (see also entry B14).]

B13 "It, Out of Darkest Jungle" [parody of filmscript]. Fantastic Stories of Imagination 13 (December):83-97, 130. [Note: Opens, "Screen treatment of an original idea by Joe Charlesville." Parody of clichés found in science fiction films.]

1973

B14 "Jacques Chrétien" [song, both words and music]. In Astounding: John W. Campbell Memorial Anthology. Edited by Harry Harrison. New York: Random House; Toronto: Random House of Canada, pp. 142, 144-46. [Note: Part of "Brothers" (A190).]

Part B: Miscellaneous Media

The NESFA Hymnal. Cambridge, Mass.: NESFA, n.d. [Note:
    Appears independent of "Brothers" (see also entry B12).]

1974

*B15 "Computers Don't Argue." [Note: Adapted by Kathleen Hamre as
    a play from the original story (see entry A152). Performed
    on three nights in January at Miami College, Richmond,
    Indiana.
    [Source: Dickson.]

    Adapted by Kathy Spencer as a play from the original story,
        and incorporated into a production called Repent Harlequin!
        [Note: Performed 10-12 February 1977, location uncon-
        firmed. Source: Dickson. Adaptation independent of
        that by Kathleen Hamre.]

B16 "Ye Prentice and ye Dragon" [poem]. Dragon-Runners' Chronicle
    [fanzine], no. 8 (December):4-7. [Note: Humorous poem in
    pseudo-Middle English. Subsequently printed by Dickson as
    a Christmas card.]

    ASF 94 (January 1975):56-62. [Note: Not listed in table
        of contents. Preceded by "The Present State of Igneos
        Research," where Dickson pretends that it is an anonymous
        poem, found in an old manuscript; included as part of this
        latter in reprints (see entry B17).]

1975

B17 "The Present State of Igneos Research" [parody of scholarly
    article]. ASF 94 (January):51-55. [Note: Introduces "Ye
    Prentice and ye Dragon" (see entry B16).]

    Ben Bova, ed. The Best of Analog. New York: Baronet
        Publishing, 1978 [paper]. [Note: Incorporates "Ye
        Prentice and ye Dragon" (see entry B16).]

B18 "A Letter to the Committee." In Resounding Haldeman Stories.
    Edited by Mike Glicksohn. [Toronto?]: Scotch Press
    Publication. [Note: Amateur publication, limited to 50
    copies. No page numbers; letter covers 7 pages including
    illustrations by various hands. Fictional satiric encounter
    with Haldeman in letter format.]

Part C: Nonfiction

C1 "Knock Twice and Ask for Morrie, or Ye Gods What a Night
    (Complete and Unexpurgated!)." <u>MFS Bulletin</u> [fanzine] 1,
    no. 5 [August 1942]:2-3. [Note: Publication of the
    Minneapolis Fantasy Society, which Dickson joined soon after
    its inception. He is mentioned frequently in the "Clubnotes"
    written by Phil Bronson (usually), until 3, no. 10 (8 March
    1943), where it is recorded that Dickson expects to be
    drafted 1 April or shortly thereafter. Issues ceased soon
    thereafter, but resumed in 1948 (see entry C7). This arti-
    cle is a humorous account of a night's drinking with
    friends.]

C2 "Fan-Scratchings." <u>MFS Bulletin</u> [fanzine] 1, no. 6 [October
    1942]:4. [Note: First appearance of a regular column on
    the activities of local fans.]

C3 "Fan-Scratchings." <u>MFS Bulletin</u> [fanzine] 2, no. 1 [November
    1942]:3-4.

C4 "Sliderule Etiquette." <u>Minnesota Technolog</u> 23 (November):53.
    [Note: Publication of the Engineering Department of the
    University of Minnesota (see also entries A3-A6). Humorous
    account of the conduct expected of undergraduate engineers.]

C5 "Fan Scratchings." <u>Fantasite</u> [fanzine] 2 (November-December):
    11-12. [Note: Column moves to another fanzine, where it
    drops the hyphen in the title. Replaces similar column by
    Joe Fortier, who moves to the spot vacated by Dickson in
    the <u>MFS Bulletin</u>. Incensed at the demotion, Fortier com-
    mences a feud against Dickson (see introduction).]

1943

C6 "Fan Scratchings." <u>Fantasite</u> [fanzine] 2 (May-June):8-10.

[Note: Last appearance of the column. "Fanta-Notes," in the next issue of Fantasite, records Dickson's entry into the armed forces.]

1948

C7   "Clubnotes." MFS Bulletin [fanzine] 4, no. 1 (January 31):5-6. [Note: First postwar publication of this fanzine, which lists Dickson as secretary-treasurer and member of the editorial board.]

C8   "Developments." MFS Bulletin [fanzine] 4, no. 1 (January 31): 3, 6. [Note: Humorous article, addressed to newer members of the Minneapolis Fantasy Society like Poul Anderson, about the prewar members' enthusiasm for drinking.]

C9   Letter to John L. Gergen in "Comments." With Phil Bronson and Manson Brackley. MFS Bulletin [fanzine] 4, no. 1 (January 31):7. [Note: Humorous warning to the publisher to ensure that they receive copies of the fanzine.]

C10   "Clubnotes." MFS Bulletin [fanzine] 4, no. 2 (February 14):4.

C11   "Clubnotes." MFS Bulletin [fanzine] 4, no. 3 (February 28):6.

C12   "Clubnotes." MFS Bulletin [fanzine] 4, no. 4 (April 28):2, 8. [Note: Since I was unable to locate subsequent issues of this fanzine, I was unable to check how long Dickson continued to write this column; presumably, he did so for the remainder of 1948 if he served one year as secretary-treasurer. The column does not appear in the March 1951 issue, the only other I was able to locate.]

1960

C13   "Half a Hoka--Poul Anderson: An Appreciation." In The Science-Fictional Sherlock Holmes. Edited by Robert C. Peterson. Denver: Council of Four, pp. 32-34. [Note: Humorous appreciation of Anderson's energy, cast in the form of dialogue between two Hokas in the roles of Sherlock Holmes and Dr. Watson. Appears with "The Adventure of the Misplaced Hound" (A32; see also entry C19).]

1961

*C14   Review of Rogue Moon, by Algis Budrys. [Source: Dickson Papers; probably appeared in a Minneapolis newspaper.]

Part C: Nonfiction

1962

*C15   Review of <u>The Sand Pebbles and Other Stories,</u> by Richard
McKenna.
[Source: Dickson Papers; probably appeared in a Minneapolis
newspaper.]

1963

C16   Review of <u>The Unwise Child,</u> by Randall Garrett.   <u>FSF</u> 24
(March):33-34.

1965

C17   "The Childe Cycle."   <u>Mirage</u> [fanzine] 2, no. 1:10-14.   [Note:
Useful explanation of the evolution of the Childe Cycle to
this date: comments upon entries A34, A96, A100, A128,
A145.]

1966

*C18   Review of <u>All Flesh Is Grass,</u> by Clifford D. Simak.   <u>Minneapolis
Sunday Tribune.</u>
[Source: Dickson.]

1968

*C19   Review of <u>The Werewolf Principle,</u> by Clifford D. Simak.
[Source: Dickson Papers; probably appeared in a Minneapolis
newspaper.]

1969

C20   "From the President, 10/18/69."   <u>SFWA Bulletin</u> 7, no. 2
[October-November 1969]:3-7.   [Note: Dickson served as
president of the Science Fiction Writers of America from
1969 to 1971.]

C21   "From the President."   <u>SFWA Bulletin</u> 7, no. 3 (December):1-9.

1970

C22   "Gordon R. Dickson."   In <u>Stella Nova: The Contemporary Science
Fiction Authors.</u>   Edited by R. Reginald.   Los Angeles:
Unicorn & Son, pp. 78-79.   [Note: Rev. ed.   <u>Contemporary</u>

Science Fiction Authors. New York: Arno Press, 1974.
Brief outline of Childe Cycle, preceded by bibliographical
and biographical data.]

R. Reginald, ed. Science Fiction and Fantasy Literature,
    vol. 2. Detroit: Gale Research, 1970.

1971

C23   PATTERSON, LEWIS. "Author to Watch Apollo Blastoff for
       'Research.'" St. Paul Sunday Pioneer Press, 24 January,
       pp. 1, 6. [Note: Interview that includes tips for begin-
       ning writers. The "research" is for "A Matter of Perspective"
       (see entry C23); experience culminated in The Far Call (see
       entry A194).]

C24   "Profile--Poul Anderson." FSF 40 (April):46-51. [Note: See
       also entry C13. Biographical profile enriched by personal
       recollections.]

       As "Poul Anderson." In The Best from Fantasy and Science
          Fiction, A Special 25th Anniversary Anthology. Edited
          by Edward L. Ferman. Garden City, N.Y.: Doubleday,
          1974.

C25   "From the President." SFWA Bulletin 6, no. 5:2. [Note: There
       is confusion over the numbering of issues. Vol. 7, nos. 2
       and 3 are whole nos. 26 and 27 (see entries C16 and C17);
       this issue is whole no. 32. See also entry C21).]

C26   "John W. Campbell, 1910-1971." SFWA Bulletin 7, no. 2:1-3.
       [Note: This issue is whole no. 35 (see entry C20). This
       memorial tribute to the great editor of ASF is Dickson's
       last official communication in the Bulletin as president of
       the SFWA. (Cf. entry A190).]

C27   "Gordon Dickson." In "Voices." Colloquy 4 (May):8. [Note:
       Along with four other writers, Dickson answers the questions:
       What is science fiction? Why do you write it? What is its
       future?]

C28   "A Matter of Perspective." ASF 88 (December):50-66. With
       Kelly Freas. [Note: Description of and reflections upon
       the launch of Apollo 14 (see also entry C18). Freas pro-
       vides five full-page illustrations.]

1973

C29   "Gordon R. Dickson: Emergency Paté; Beef Short Ribs with Egg

Noodles." In Cooking Out of this World. Edited by Anne
McCaffrey. New York: Ballantine Books, pp. 61-63 [paper].
[Note: Two recipes contributed by Dickson to this cook-
book.]

C30 "Notes on the Childe Cycle." OAFS [fanzine] 1, no. 2:6-12.
[Note: As well as covering additional material, comments
more fully upon the philosophical basis of the cycle than
does "The Childe Cycle," which appeared in 1965 (see entry
C17).]

1974

C31 "Plausibility in Science Fiction" [article]. In Science
Fiction, Today and Tomorrow. Edited by Reginald Bretnor.
New York, Evanston, San Francisco, and London: Harper &
Row, pp. 295-308. Reprint. Penguin, 1975. [Note: Dates
cited in the select bibliography of Dickson's writings are
unreliable.]

1975

C32 "Ten Years of Nebula Awards" [article]. In Nebula Award
Stories Ten. Edited by James E. Gunn. New York, Evanston,
San Francisco, and London: Harper & Row, pp. 97-104.

C33 Introduction to Combat SF. Garden City, N.Y.: Doubleday,
pp. vii-ix. [Note: See entry A203.]

C34 MacVICAR, WILLIAM. "They Don't Sniff at Science Fiction
Writers Now" [interview]. Toronto Globe and Mail,
14 August, p. 11.

C35 "Pros and Cons." Rune [fanzine] 7, no. 7:17-21. [Note: Text
of guest-of-honor speech at Minicon 10, held in Minneapolis.
Expresses appreciation of constructive criticism and support
given a writer by fans.]

C36 Introduction to Three to Dorsai! Garden City, N.Y.: Nelson
Doubleday. [Note: Outlines structure of Childe Cycle (see
also entries A205, C15, C25).]

*C37 "Interview with Gordon R. Dickson." S-S-F [fanzine].
[Source: Dickson Papers, which note that the interview was
conducted 15 September.]

Part C: Nonfiction

1976

C38   SCHWEITZER, DARRELL. "Gordon Dickson" [interview]. In SF
       Voices. Baltimore: T-K Graphics, pp. 57–63. [Note: One
       of a collection of interviews by Schweitzer. Primarily
       discusses the Childe Cycle.]

C39   "Excalibur Interviews: Gordon R. Dickson." Excalibur
       [fanzine] 1, no. 1:23–33.

C40   LUNDQUIST, BARB. "For Gordon R. Dickson, Responsibility,
       Fantasy Join in Science Fiction." Richfield Sun, 17
       November, p. 10. [Note: Interview in Minneapolis news-
       paper.]

*C41   Review of Millenium, by Ben Bova.
       [Source: Dickson Papers, which note that it was written
       in March 1976 (probably for a Minneapolis newspaper?).]

C42   BANKS, MICHAEL A. "A Short Interview with Gordon R. Dickson."
       ERG Quarterly, no. 57 (January):5–7.

C43   STEINFELDT, LEE. "Says Science Fiction Writers Should Publish
       Themselves" [interview]. Syracuse Post-Standard, 5 February,
       p. 6.

C44   Introduction to Futurelove: A Science Fiction Triad. [Edited
       by Roger Elwood.] Indianapolis and New York: Bobbs-Merrill,
       pp. vii–x.

*C45   SHARE, TODD. "An Interview with Gordon R. Dickson." Yonder
       [fanzine] (May).
       [Source: Dickson Papers.]

C46   FRASER, BRIAN M. "Interstellar Probe: Gordon R. Dickson
       Interview." Galileo: Magazine of Science and Fiction, no.
       5 (October):6–12. [Note: Discusses future space explora-
       tion.]

C47   "Gordon R. Dickson: SFans and the Future of Society." Jinnia
       Clan Journal [fanzine], Winter, pp. 8–9. [Note: Text of
       guest-of-honor speech at Rivercon III.]

C48   "Readers Pick Their Most Memorable Books of the Year. Gordon
       R. Dickson." Minneapolis Tribune, 4 December, p. 11S.
       [Note: Notes value of Hendrick Smith's The Russians for
       final revisions of The Far Call (A194).]

Part C: Nonfiction

1978

C49   Introduction to Nebula Winners Twelve. New York, Hagerstown,
       San Francisco, and London: Harper & Row, pp. ix–xiii.

C50   "Poul Anderson's Saga." In Leprecon IV Programme [pp. 3–6].
       [Notes: Conference in Phoenix, Arizona, 17–19 March; pages
       unnumbered; illustrations by Ken Fletcher. Lighthearted
       brief appreciation of Anderson's career in comic format.]

C51   "SF: Shaper of Twentieth Century Literature." Minnesota
       Technolog 58 (Spring I):8–9. [Note: Dickson returns to the
       magazine of the Engineering Department of the University of
       Minnesota, where he published as an undergraduate thirty-six
       years earlier (see entries A3–6, C4). Contends that science
       fiction attracts bright literary talent because it grants
       freedom to express new ideas.]

C52   MIESEL, SANDRA. "Algol Interview: Gordon R. Dickson." Algol:
       The Magazine about Science Fiction 15 (Spring):33–38. [Note:
       First of several articles by the critic, whom Dickson has
       praised for her insights into his work.]

C53   Foreword to Home from the Shore. New York: Ace, pp. 9–13.
       [Note: See entry A137. Appears in Ace illustrated edition
       of 1979 only. Stresses importance of integrated relation-
       ship between illustration and story.]

C54   Letter to Richard E. Geis. Science Fiction Review [fanzine] 7
       (July):44–45. [Note: Letter dated 19 May 1978. Predicts
       "Neo-Puritan revolution" in America before end of century.]

C55   McMURRAY, CLIFFORD. "An Interview with Gordon R. Dickson."
       Science Fiction Review [fanzine] 7 (July):6–12.

C56   BANKS, MICHAEL A. "SF Prediction: Speculation or Future
       Fact?" Starlog: The Magazine of the Future, no. 15
       (August):61–63. [Note: Cites predictions by several au-
       thors, including Dickson.]

1979

C57   MARTIN, D.R. "Conversations with Three Who Write 'Sci-Fi':
       Frederick Pohl, Clifford D. Simak, and Gordon R. Dickson
       Talk about Their Work." Northliner 11 (February):51–53.
       [Note: Trade magazine from North Central, (now Republic)
       Airlines.]

Part C: Nonfiction

1980

*C58   MIESEL, SANDRA. "A Conversation with Gordon R. Dickson."
        Runway 37 [fanzine], no. 5. (Summer):8-10.
        [Source: Author's tearsheets.]

Part D: Critical Studies

1943

D1   BRONSON, PHIL? [SQUANCHFOOT, pseud.]. "MFS Members As Seen by
         Squanchfoot." Fantasite [fanzine] 2, no. 5 (May-June):13-14.
             Brief biographical sketch of Dickson as a nineteen-year-
         old science fiction fan, listing his tastes and interests.
         Notes his intention "one day to write textbooks for the
         courses in science-fiction that University English Depart-
         ments will have to give."

1956

D2   BOUCHER, ANTHONY. "Recommended Reading." FSF 10 (April):79.
             Review of Alien from Arcturus: Story "light-weight and
         familiar . . . but distinguished by the delightful presence
         of the Alien (Peep), a furiously gentle creature of comic
         dignity."

D3   _____. "Recommended Reading." FSF 11 (September):109.
             Review of Mankind on the Run: Formula plot, but handled
         with "fresh ingenuity and genuinely surprising melodramatic
         twists." Praises both background details and "an odd sort
         of mysticism which is Dickson's own."

D4   KNIGHT, DAMON. "Infinity's Choice." Infinity Science Fiction
         1 (August):107.
             Review of Alien from Arcturus: Conventional story re-
         deemed by "good-natured but wacky sense of humor." Peep is
         "the most engaging extraterrestrial in recent memory--and
         the funniest bar none."

D5   MILLER, P. SCHUYLER. "The Reference Library." ASF 57 (July):
         160.
             Review of Alien from Arcturus: "No world-beater but I
         liked [it]." The alien Peep is "delightful . . . plenty of
         fun."

D6   _____. "The Reference Library." ASF 58 (November):157.
        Review of Mankind on the Run: "Plots are downright Van
        Vogtian . . . basic gimmick is stated and demonstrated but
        never made reasonable. Some of the details are very well
        done . . . but the book as a whole doesn't quite come off."

                                1958

D7   BOUCHER, ANTHONY. "Recommended Reading." FSF 14 (April):95.
        Review of Earthman's Burden: "A gleeful book of sf
      (which in this case stands for satiric frolic)."

D8   GALE, FLOYD C. "Galaxy's 5 Star Shelf." Galaxy 16 (May):
        117-18.
        Review of Earthman's Burden: When read separately with
      time lapses, some of the tales are "reasonably amusing,"
      but "the cumulative effect is less rewarding."

D9   KNIGHT, DAMON. "Infinity's Choice." Infinity Science Fiction
        3 (March):60-61.
        Review of Earthman's Burden. [Note: Title erroneously
      given as Earthman's Return.] In spite of "some overcute
      writing," the stories are "pretty funny." Plots "are noth-
      ing much; the stories stand or fall on the Hokas as the
      medium for burlesque."

D10   MILLER, P. SCHUYLER. "The Reference Library." ASF 61 (April):
        143-44.
        Review of Earthman's Burden: "These hapless rollicking
      tales have all the subtlety of Laurel and Hardy, but they
      have enough variety, and have been hitched together deftly
      enough . . . that they don't pall."

D11   STURGEON, THEODORE. Review of Earthman's Burden. Venture 2
        (January):80.
        Tales "range from hilarious to cute."

                                1960

D12   BESTER, ALFRED. "Books." FSF 19 (November):93.
        Review of The Genetic General: "A swinging piece of
      space opera . . . well-written . . . most satisfying."

D13   COTTS, S.E. "The Spectroscope." Amazing Science Fiction
        Stories 34 (October):135-36.
        Review of The Genetic General: Admires the craftsmanship
      that makes the story "both convincing and interesting," and
      the "half dozen memorable characters" through whom "the
      reader gets a picture of what makes that far-flung universe
      workable" in a "first-rate action story."

D14 POHL, FREDERIK. "Book Reviews by Frederik Pohl." WIF 10
(November):83-84.
Review of The Genetic General and Time to Teleport:
Considers author an uneven writer, but The Genetic General
is "a fine, moving, exciting book," showing Dickson "at the
top of his form." The hero's character is developed well,
and though the galactic culture is improbable, "by a sleight
of hand he tricks us into suspension of disbelief." Time to
Teleport is also about a mutant threat, "but here the piece
falls apart in our hands."

1961

D15 GALE, FLOYD C. "Galaxy's 5 Star Shelf." Galaxy 19 (August):
157.
Review of Secret under the Sea: "Action far outpaces
plot," but should appeal to youngsters.

D16 GAREY, DOROTHY. Review of Secret Under the Sea. LJ 86
(March):1322.
Praises the "convincing details concerning man's use of
the oceans." Plot adequate, if predictable.

D17 MILLER, P. SCHUYLER. "The Reference Library." ASF 67 (July):
155.
Review of The Genetic General and Time to Teleport: In
The Genetic General, "the author does a fine job of changing
the rather insufferable young man of the early chapters into
a plausible master mind near the end." Time to Teleport
"reads like a first tentative exploration of the 'Dorsai'
theme," but the story, though "full of fascinating concepts,"
is "tangled."

1962

D18 GALE, FLOYD C. "Galaxy's 5 Star Shelf." Galaxy 21 (December):
194.
Review of Naked to the Stars: "Cracking good war story
. . . Dickson makes his readers absorbedly aware that service in an organization dedicated to peace can require far
more courage than mere combat."

D19 MILLER, P. SCHUYLER. "The Reference Library." ASF 69 (May):
169-70.
Review of Delusion World and Spacial Delivery: Enjoys
the humor in Delusion World, and finds the hero's method of
getting out of the mess he gets himself into "novel and interesting." Spacial Delivery has "basted adventure with
humor." Dilbians are Hokas grown large, complete with "pro-
testing hero" again, but the story is confusing.

D20   _____. "The Reference Library." <u>ASF</u> 69 (June):161-62.
        Review of <u>Naked to the Stars</u>: Answer to <u>Starship</u>
<u>Troopers</u> by Heinlein and worthy of a Hugo. Shows how dif-
ferent war can be when a nation and a race grow up.

D21   _____. "The Reference Library." <u>ASF</u> 70 (October):167-68.
        Review of <u>Necromancer</u>: Conclusion ties up the various
strands of the plot, but this remains a confusing and "puz-
zling" book with a "Van Vogtian plot."

D22   _____. "The Reference Library." <u>ASF</u> 68 (January):156-57.
        Review of <u>Secret under the Sea</u>: Story has hero with whom
children can identify, a strange and wonderful pet, "a marvellous undersea world, and its plot grows out of that world
and conditions there. . . . Good science fiction."

                              1963

D23   GARRETT, RANDAL. "Books." <u>FSF</u> 24 (March):34-36.
        Review of <u>Necromancer</u>: A "Van Vogtian novel" with many
imaginative ideas, almost all of which are "thrown away" in
order to move on to the next one. "The action is fast and
well-paced; the futuristic science is well thought out; the
philosophy is deep and perceptive." However, many mysterious
loose ends remain.

D24   WILLIAMS, PAUL. Review of <u>Secret under Antarctica</u>. <u>LJ</u> 88
        (15 November):4474.
        More adventure than science fiction, but "not particularly
notable as either; characters stock, story thin, but enjoyable enough."

                              1964

D25   MILLER, P. SCHUYLER. "The Reference Library." <u>ASF</u> 73 (May):
        88.
        Review of <u>Secret under Antarctica</u>: Dickson livens a good
adventure yarn "with novel twists and legitimate scientific
speculation."

                              1965

D26   ANON. Review of <u>Space Winners</u>. <u>KR</u> 33 (1 November):1121-22.
        The adventure is "not very convincing," and the aliens
"seem pretty foolish." However, the three teenagers are
"quite believable in their actions, reactions and conversations, and help make up for weaknesses in the story."

D27   BOATWRIGHT, TALIAFERRO. "Getting Along Swimmingly." Book
       Week, 28 March, p. 19.
           Review of Secret under the Caribbean, which puts emphasis
       upon scientific "trappings." Thus "though the background is
       well researched, the story is paper thin, and the characters
       flat as cartoons."

D28   MERRIL, JUDITH. "Books." FSF 28 (May):70-75.
           Review of The Alien Way: a successful morality play.
       The "detailed study of one rarely xenophiliac human engaged
       in a near-killing conflict of identification with himself
       and the alien is fascinating." Demonstration that physio-
       logical characteristics affect cultural ethos is more tedi-
       ous.

                              1966

D29   ANON. Review of Space Winners. Booklist 62 (1 April):774.
           A convincingly related tale with interesting sidelights
       on moral and cultural values.

D30   JONES, DOROTHY S. Review of Space Winners. LJ 91 (15 January):
       432-33.
           Praises the book as "good adventuresome reading with
       moral overtones."

D31   MADSEN, ALAN. "In the Future Tense." Book Week, 27 February,
       p. 10.
           Review of Space Winners: Protagonists learn "the moral
       value of having done it oneself, the cultural value of
       learning the use of discovery, and cognitive value of a
       sound structure of knowledge." Yet the novel is more than
       "a mere sociological tract" because action arises out of
       character, and the characters are credible, particularly
       Jim and alien Peep.

D32   MERRIL, JUDITH. "Books." FSF 30 (March):46-47.
           Review of Mission to Universe: Explores the personality
       of a hero-leader who "feels himself set apart from others,
       whose ego-satisfactions have narrowed into the puritan range
       of 'rightness' and 'respect' and 'responsibility.'" Good
       as far as it goes, but avoids full implications of character.

D33   MILLER, P. SCHUYLER. "The Reference Library." ASF 77 (May):
       154.
           Review of Space Winners: "Excellent juvenile SF."
       Dickson displays same care he shows in adult work.

D34   Van DEVENTER, MARY LOU. Review of Space Winners. English
       Journal 55 (May):616-17.

Praises the plot, "vivid" characterization, and "psycho-
logical verisimilitude."

1967

D35   ANON. "A Conquered World." Times Literary Supplement, 25 May,
      p. 459.
         Review of Space Winners: The story is "thoughtful and
      original," but the characters never become "impressive as
      people. This is a difficulty built into the structure of
      science-fiction. . . . Although it is not always easy to
      understand where the story is going, there are memorable
      episodes," mostly involving the "endearing" alien Peep.

D36   ANON. Review of Soldier, Ask Not. PW, 5 June, p. 180.
         Considers the novel too ambitious; "imaginative but it's
      hard to identify with anybody in the story. And the florid,
      pretentious prose is frequently plain hard reading."

D37   BLISHEN, EDWARD. "Children's Books: For the Almost Old."
      Listener, 18 May, p. 661.
         Review of Space Winners. Considers that "a sort of highly
      intelligent weirdness is the keynote."

D38   GARDNER, AURORA W. Review of Planet Run. LJ 92 (July):2606.
         The novel is really an old-fashioned western despite
      science fiction trappings, but satisfactory as neither.

D39   WHITE, TED. "Books." FSF 33 (October):31-33.
         Review of The Space Swimmers: Too ambitious and melo-
      dramatic. Intuitive function is reduced to the level of
      "another comic-book super-power, unexplained, convenient,
      and unbelievable." Grand ideas are presented in an "obso-
      lete" and imprecise style.

1968

D40   MILLER, P. SCHUYLER. "The Reference Library." ASF 81
      (April):163.
         Review of Soldier, Ask Not: Inferior to Dorsai! and
      Necromancer, perhaps because the antihero is hard to like.
      Dickson's future universe has grown very complex. "Read
      the book for its ideas, if not for its story."

D41   _____. "The Reference Library." ASF 81 (May):167.
         Review of The Space Swimmers. Appreciates the "mechanism
      of alternate isolation and amalgamation as a basic force in
      evolving. . . . Social forces and racial powers must operate
      through individuals, and so the pattern of the book works

itself out in an intricate play of personalities. It
should be an award contender."

1969

D42   ANON. Review of Danger--Human. KR 37 (15 November):1228.
       Reprint. KR 37 (1 December):1276.
       "A genuine finishing touch" in these varied and "con-
       sistently entertaining" stories.

D43   ANON. Review of Danger--Human. PW, 29 December, p. 61.
       Considers all the stories good, "Dolphin's Way" and
       "Lulungomeena" outstanding.

D44   ANON. Review of None but Man. Booklist 65 (15 July):1262.
       Admires the "fast-paced adventure."

D45   ANON. Review of None but Man." KR 37 (1 February):140.
       The hero's exploration of alien mores makes for a very
       good story.

D46   ANON. Review of None but Man. PW, 27 January, p. 91.
       "Well written," but "talky and a bit on the tedious
       side."

D47   ANON. Review of Spacepaw. KR 37 (1 January):9.
       "Altogether enough funny scenes and dialogue to make
       Spacepaw one of the happier five finger exercises."

D48   ANON. Review of Wolfling. PW, 28 April, p. 89.
       Smoothly plotted and written; well-paced action. "Good
       entertainment all the way, but of the non-subtle razzle-
       dazzle kind."

D49   HAYNES, ELIZABETH. Review of Spacepaw. LJ 94 (15 March):1338.
       Amusing and "zestful." "Some confusion in the story line
       and the forced love interest are offset by the rising sus-
       pense and entertainment."

D50   MILLER, P. SCHUYLER. "The Reference Library." ASF 84
       (October):172-73.
       Review of None but Man: Despite its "lively action . . .
       stressing the relativity of right and wrong," this is not
       one of Dickson's better novels.

D51   _____. "The Reference Library." ASF 84 (November):170.
       Review of Spacepaw: "A lively unpretentious yarn" about
       mankind's attempt "to find a modus vivendi with an alien
       race."

D52   SCHUMAN, PATRICIA. Review of None but Man. LJ 94 (1 April):
      1518.
            The novel raises an interesting sociological question:
      "Can man possibly relate to a totally alien frame of refer-
      ence? . . . Recommended."

                              1970

D53   ANON. Review of Danger--Human. Booklist 66 (15 May):1139.
            "Well-crafted, consistently appealing tales deal with
      man's association with other intelligent life forms."

D54   ANON. Review of Hour of the Horde. KR 38 (1 February):134.
            "A fast hour's diversion if you can deal with the author's
      contention that our more murderous impulses are not only
      necessary but laudable."

D55   ANON. Review of Hour of the Horde. KR 38 (1 August):804.
            The hero of the novel "defines overdrive as hysterical
      strength, and however you construe hysterical, it fits
      here."

D56   ANON. Review of Mutants. KR 38 (1 March):280-81.
            "View ranges from the nihilistic to the poetic positive
      and it is consistently in focus."

D57   ANON. Review of Mutants. PW, 23 February, p. 151.
            Most stories are "well-constructed studies of character."

D58   BLISH, JAMES. "Books." FSF 39 (September):19-20.
            Review of "Jean Duprès." Praises skillful use of sus-
      pense.

D59   CALVALLINI, JEAN. Review of Danger--Human. LJ 95 (15 May):1969.
            A "speculative" collection about "man's constant search
      for meaning in his existence." Tales of "uniformly high
      quality give much to enjoy and ponder."

D60   CONNELLY, WAYNE. Review of Spacepaw. Science Fiction Review
      [fanzine] 41 (November):29-30.
            Perceives two plots: the conflict with the Dilbians and
      a "tortuous spy-plot." Appreciates the humor, which is
      "slow, objective, gentle, and warmly tolerant" in this
      "space-age animal fable."

*D61 GODDARD, J. Review of None but Man. Cypher [fanzine] 1
      (June):8.
            [Source: Hall, SFBRI 5 (1974):11.]

D62   LAITE, BERKLEY. Review of Danger--Human. LJ 95 (1 January):82.

Appreciates the "considerable care in smoothly developing plots and characters. . . . In each story Homo sapiens is a direct threat to the survival of an ET/self."

D63 MICHALIK, ANNE P. Review of Hour of the Horde. LJ 95 (15 October):3635-36.
"Below average . . . marred by a slow beginning, weak characterizations, and little excitement or suspense."

D64 MINES, S. Review of Spacepaw. Luna Monthly [fanzine], no. 12 (May):30.
Scornfully dismisses novel as a comic book "space western" with dialogue at a nine-year-old level.

D65 PATTEN, FRED. Review of Earthman's Burden. Science Fiction Review [fanzine] 39 (August):22.
Considers Hoka stories "practically the last examples of pure humor we've had in sf on a regular basis." Well-written connecting material allows the book to be read as a novel or a collection of short stories.

D66 POLACHEK, JANET G. Review of Mutants. LJ 95 (15 June):2284.
"Excellent action stories for most part"; "Home from the Shore" is "almost a masterpiece."

D67 RAPKIN, J. Review of None but Man. Luna Monthly [fanzine], no. 9 (February):26.
A highly recommended treatment of the familiar themes of colonial revolt against unsympathetic authority and alien-human conflict.

D68 SEARLES, BAIRD. "For Young Readers." New York Times Book Review, 20 September, p. 47.
Review of Hour of the Horde: "Mushy metaphysics and total lack of subtlety will make this unpalatable for all but the most unquestioning."

D69 WALKER, PAUL. Review of Danger--Human. Science Fiction Review [fanzine] 40 (October):31.
Praises this "nice approach" to an interesting theme, but focuses on "simple" characterization, "sloppily described" backgrounds, and "plodding" pace.

1971

D70 ANON. Review of Sleepwalker's World. Booklist 68 (1 December): 319.
"Fast-moving adventure tale of good against evil."

D71 ANON. Review of Sleepwalker's World. KR 39 (15 June):656.

Reprint. 39 (1 July):688.
An interesting parable of good versus evil.

D72   ANON. Review of Sleepwalker's World. PW, 7 June, p. 51.
Appreciates the expert handling of melodrama and suspense.

D73   ANON. Review of The Tactics of Mistake. KR 39 (1 February):
140.
"The logistics are consistently interesting."

D74   ANON. Review of The Tactics of Mistake. PW, 1 February, p. 68.
Praises the novel as "smooth and exciting." It's "fascinating to watch the ingenious workings of Colonel Grahame's
mind as he shines as soldier and politician in midst of col-
orful and original off-earth societies."

D75   BELL, THOMAS R. Review of The Tactics of Mistake. LJ 96
(15 March):979.
Despite "disbelief" and a sometimes overly complicated
plot, the story is an absorbing combination of bold character and serious thought.

D76   BUDRYS, ALGIS. "Galaxy Bookshelf." Galaxy 32 (September-
October):146-47.
Review of The Tactics of Mistake: Though weak on motiva-
tion and probability, the book has strong appeal: "There is
no denying the power of this kind of storytelling."

D77   del REY, LESTER. "Reading Room." WIF 21 (November-December):
173-74.
Review of The Tactics of Mistake: Considers both hero
and heroine more believable than their counterparts in The
Genetic General. Novel "a thoroughly good adventure story
with some depth."

D78   ELLISON, HARLAN. "Books." FSF 40 (June):22-23.
Review of Mutants: Admires "the strong emotional content
in Dickson's work; always cerebral, yet not overbearingly
so," and the "unerring perception and honesty." Suggests
perceptively that the author is not more highly regarded because his work, though always of the first rank, is too often
limited by mundaneness and fondness for the conventional elements of the genre.

D79   GILLESPIE, BRUCE R. "The Original Science Fiction Anthologies."
SF Commentary [fanzine], no. 21 (May):28-30.
Review of "Jean Duprès." Appreciates the parable of conflict between civilization and a smart child, with the narrator helpless to intervene.

D80   HALTERMAN, D. Review of Spacepaw. Son of WSFA Journal

[fanzine], no. 19 (April):8.
Complains of the tendency "to explain everything," but finds the Dilbians "fascinating creatures . . . Hokas grown up." Enjoyable book.

D81   MILLER, P. SCHUYLER. "The Reference Library." ASF 87 (May): 163-64.
Review of Mutants: A fine collection of stories "dedicated to the faith that we have not stopped evolving" and will adapt to any situation we create. Yet the mutants are "men, and find it hard to forget it."

D82   _____. "The Reference Library." ASF 88 (December):167.
Review of Sleepwalker's World: Too "gimmicky" and conventional. Only the wolf is memorable.

D83   _____. "The Reference Library." ASF 88 (October):168.
Review of The Tactics of Mistake: The hero is ruthless because he is pragmatic, and "so close to an automaton in working out his plans, the book never really captures the reader emotionally." Considers Dickson's future history logical and humanly real, with a strong philosophical foundation.

D84   NEWTON, J. Review of Mutants. Son of WSFA Journal [fanzine], no. 21 (May):5.
Appreciates "life and plausibility. . . . It's good reading."

D85   PASKOW, D. Review of Danger--Human! Luna Monthly [fanzine], no. 21 (February):29.
Impressed by author's "evocative capabilities" describing "the life forms and social structures of alien societies and the bumbling attempts of Earthmen to fit in."

D86   _____. Review of Hour of the Horde. Luna Monthly [fanzine], no. 30 (November):29.
"Blood and thunder space opera. . . . No message here."

D87   PAULS, T. Review of The Tactics of Mistake. WSFA Journal [fanzine], no. 78 (August-October):25-26.
Considers the story implausible and contrived, but enjoyable because it moves fast enough to get away with it.

D88   POST, J.B. Review of Sleepwalker's World. LJ 96 (July):2351.
Although the plot structure is weak, the story as a whole reads well, and the future society is interestingly depicted.

Part D: Critical Studies

1972

D89   ANON. Review of The Outposter. KR 40 (15 May):602.
           Grumbles that were the brilliant young hero "not such a
       tiresome, graceless clod, one might applaud his feats."
       Heavy-handed work.

D90   ANON. Review of The Outposter. PW, 29 May, p. 33.
           "Full of action and quite believable."

D91   ANON. Review of The Pritcher Mass. KR 40 (15 July):825. Re-
           print. KR 40 (1 August):869.
               "Old-fashioned approach to a newfangled subject--the plot
       keeps you guessing, the characters don't."

D92   ANON. Review of The Pritcher Mass. PW, 24 July, p. 74.
           "A taut, suspenseful story that makes the mental gymnas-
       tics in the tale easy to take."

D93   ANON. Review of Sleepwalker's World. Center for Children's
           Books (Chicago) Bulletin 25 (March):105.
               "Writing style is vigorous, and the story has action and
       suspense enough to compensate for the extravagances of the
       plot."

*D94   BERMAN, RUTH. "Division Mars Dickson Story." Minneapolis
           Tribune, 17 September.
               [Source: Clipping of review collected in Dickson
       Papers.] Review of The Outposter: The two main plot lines
       are not reconciled, and the characters are not fully
       developed.

D95   BLISH, JAMES. "Books." FSF 42 (June):97.
               Review of Sleepwalker's World: Praises Dickson as a
       writer for "clear and efficient" prose, gift for storytell-
       ing, and "bardic feeling for the evils, nobilities and tra-
       gedies of human existence." This novel is in some respects
       frightening, but concludes on typically optimistic note.

D96   _____. "Books." FSF 42 (February):37-38.
               Review of The Tactics of Mistake: "A carefully crafted
       action story" that retains interest despite "lack of sus-
       pense," but lacks real "substance."

D97   CONNELLY, WAYNE. " . . . Whose Game Was Empires." Riverside
           Quarterly 5 (August):224-25.
               Review of The Tactics of Mistake: Despite "clever" plot-
       ting, the narrative structure is flawed, so that the story
       falls into two parts. This division is emphasized by a
       change in style and tempo. A fascinating character study
       of the hero, whose "intense rationalism and cold-heartedness"
       render him almost "monstrous" by the end of the novel.

D98   del REY, LESTER. "Reading Room." <u>WIF</u> 21 (November–December):
       157–58.
            Review of <u>The Outposter</u>: Appreciates "Dickson's deep in-
       terest in the way the past must affect the future," "his
       always ingenious handling of the sociology of aliens," and
       the "exploration of the values of outcasts from one culture
       when exposed to a different one."

D99   POST, J.B. Review of <u>The Pritcher Mass</u>. <u>LJ</u> 97 (August):2641.
       Written well and entertainingly.

D100   RICHTER, JOYCE. Review of <u>The Outposter</u>. <u>LJ</u> 97 (August):2651.
            Considers the characters well developed and the author's
       ideas on the acceptance of a hero in society to be added
       dimensions in this action-filled novel.

D101   WALKER, P. Review of <u>Sleepwalker's World</u>. <u>Luna Monthly</u>
       [fanzine] 38–39 (July–August):56.
            Dismisses the novel as fun, but little else: background
       sketchy, hero brainless, villains foolish.

                              1973

D102   ANON. Review of <u>Alien Art</u>. <u>Center for Children's Books
       (Chicago) Bulletin</u> 27 (October):25.
            Important issues implicit in the book tend to "cloud the
       story, which moves at an uneven pace" despite its vigor.
       The protagonist is "almost a caricature of the strong, taci-
       turn, resourceful pioneer."

D103   ANON. Review of <u>Alien Art</u>. <u>KR</u> 41 (1 April):395–96.
            The novel has "the moral certainties and tough talk of
       the old-fashioned western."

D104   ANON. Review of <u>The Outposter</u>. <u>Booklist</u> 69 (1 January):428.
            Praises the "fast-paced story."

D105   ANON. Review of <u>The Pritcher Mass</u>. <u>Booklist</u> 69 (1 January):
       429.
            The story is "intricate and suspenseful."

D106   ANON. Review of <u>The R-Master</u>. <u>KR</u> 41 (15 September):1057.
            "Energetically suspenseful," though the intriguing premise
       of an intelligence-enhancing drug might have been more fully
       developed."

D107   ANON. Review of <u>The R-Master</u>. <u>PW</u>, 24 September, pp. 181–82.
            Despite "moderate suspense," the novel is not entirely
       satisfying: "believable and interesting effects of the
       drug" are offset by "unconvincing worldwide conspiracy."

D108   ANON. Review of The Star Road. KR 41 (15 February):214.
       Considers the collection "professional," but "old-
       fashioned" and "slightly flat."

D109   ANON. Review of The Star Road. PW, 26 February, p. 122.
       "Old-fashioned science fiction," where "patriotism, team
       loyalty and the romance of space are ever present." Several
       stories are "marred by rather inadequate endings tacked onto
       ingenious and well-developed premises."

D110   ANDERSON, POUL. "In Re: Gordon R. Dickson." OAFS [fanzine]
       1, no. 2:1-3.
       Personal appreciation by an old friend.

D111   DAVIDSON, AVRAM. "Books." FSF 44 (April):37-38.
       Review of The Pritcher Mass: Considers that Dickson has
       not "ever written a sloppy line." Though vague on the na-
       ture of the mass, the author "succeeds in suspending dis-
       belief." However, the novel is "conventional and far-
       fetched."

D112   del REY, LESTER. "Reading Room." WIF 21 (February):163-65.
       Review of "Things Which Are Caesar's" and The Pritcher
       Mass: In the former, "the cast of characters is rich and
       well integrated. . . . Dickson's execution is done surely
       and well." The latter is "far below Dickson's usual high
       level": though the "basic idea is strong," the resolution
       is contrived.

D113   FREDSTROM, B. Review of The Tactics of Mistake. Luna Monthly
       [fanzine], no. 46 (March):16.
       Praises this fine science fiction adventure tale, with
       more depth than the usual novel of action.

D114   HARRISON, DEBORAH. Review of The Star Road. LJ 98 (15 April):
       1307.
       Finds "no startlingly new ideas, but tales are well-
       written and hold the reader's attention."

D115   HAYNES, ELIZABETH. Review of Alien Art. LJ 98 (July):2192.
       "The symbolism is obvious here, but the characterization
       and plot are good."

D116   MILLER, P. SCHUYLER. "The Reference Library." ASF 90
       (January):164-65.
       Review of The Outposter: Notes parallels with America's
       achieving independence. Story told in terms of the people
       who lived it.

D117   _____. "The Reference Library." ASF 92 (November):169-70.
       Review of The Pritcher Mass: Does not consider this one

of Dickson's better efforts: the author explores outer
space more successfully than "inner space."

D118   PATTERSON, BILL. "Gordon R. Dickson: A Reader's Appreciation."
        OAFS [fanzine] 1, no. 2:4-5.
            Brief observations on the importance of theme in Dickson's
        novels.

D119   POST, J.B. Review of The Pritcher Mass. Luna Monthly
        [fanzine], no. 44 (January):32.
            "Top drawer entertainment," though the ending is "a
        trifle disappointing."

D120   RICHEY, C. Review of Sleepwalker's World. Kliatt Paperback
        Book Guide 7 (April):81.
            Deserves high praise, for it "melds the usual sci-fi
        atmosphere with the convincing depiction of a resourceful
        and self-reliant hero."

D121   STURGEON, THEODORE. "Galaxy Bookshelf." Galaxy 33 (March-
        April):155-56.
            Review of The Pritcher Mass: Praises this interesting
        and legitimate approach to witchcraft, and its grim warning
        about the environment.

D122   _____. "Galaxy Bookshelf." Galaxy 34 (September):88.
            Review of The Star Road: Praises this collection of
        "fine stories" by "one of the better, reliable storytellers
        around." "On Messenger Mountain" particularly "builds up a
        thrumming tension."

                                1974

D123   ANON. Review of Ancient, My Enemy. KR 42 (15 August):903.
            "Dickson's at his best with social science fiction like
        the three stories in this collection that deal with human
        attempts to cope with an alien species in an alien environ-
        ment." Though sometimes pedestrian, tales are usually in-
        ventive.

D124   ANON. Review of Gremlins, Go Home! Center for Children's
        Books (Chicago) Bulletin 28 (September):5.
            This fantasy is "often silly, and not quite convincing
        in its logic, although it's lots of fun. . . . The gremlins'
        conversations are a bit on the cute side, but the references
        to their culture . . . are intriguing."

D125   ANON. Review of Gremlins, Go Home! KR 42 (1 January):4-5.
            Considers that "too much depends on sight gags and silly
        accents," but that the character of the protagonist arouses
        some interest.

Part D: Critical Studies

D126   ANON. Review of Gremlins, Go Home! PW, 21 January, p. 87.
        A deft fantasy with plenty of laughs and charm.

D127   ANON. Review of The R-Master. Booklist 70 (1 March):717.
        The story is "taut, fast-paced, thought provoking."

D128   ANON. Review of The R-Master. Booklist 70 (15 March):801.
        Review of The R-Master: "Pits unique individual against
        the oppressor. . . . Intriguing fare."

D129   BRADY, MARY LOU. Review of Gremlins, Go Home! LJ 99
        (15 September):2265.
        The story is "far-fetched, a bit wordy, and overdone in
        the accent department . . . but kids will certainly enjoy
        the heaping dose of humor."

*D130   D'AMMASSA, D. Review of The R-Master. Son of WSFA Journal
        [fanzine], no. 132 (March):3.
        [Source: Hall, SFBRI 5 (1974):11.]

D131   GEIS, RICHARD E. "The Geisorcist's Woes." Science Fiction
        Review (The Alien Critic) [fanzine] 9 (May):40.
        Review of Mutants: Considers Dickson a "better writer
        of the short forms than of novels." Approves of his "wide
        range of themes," and the balance between "basic sympathy
        and humanity" and "brutal realities and harsh philosophy."

D132   ____. "Staggering Losses . . . Retreat Impossible . . . God
        Help Us, Here He Comes Again - - -." Science Fiction Review
        (The Alien Critic) [fanzine] 9 (May):36.
        Review of The R-Master: "Dickson does a good job of sus-
        pense/mystery writing," but the topic is well worn.

*D133   GOLDFRANK, J. Review of Ancient, My Enemy. Son of WSFA
        Journal [fanzine], nos. 163-164 (October):7.
        [Source: Hall, SFBRI 5 (1974):11.]

*D134   LAMPTON, C. Review of The R-Master. Son of WSFA Journal
        [fanzine], nos. 161-162 (October):3-4.
        [Source: Hall, SFBRI 5 (1974):11.]

*D135   McCAULEY, KIRBY. "New Fiction." Minneapolis Tribune, 13
        January.
        [Source: Clipping of review collected in Dickson
        Papers.] Review of The R-Master: Appreciative short analy-
        sis of thematic significance.

D136   MATTERN, P. Review of The Pritcher Mass. Kliatt Paperback
        Book Guide 8 (February):93.
        An unusual and entertaining combination, in that the
        "technological advance is one of ESP," and witches and war-
        locks play a part.

D137   MINES, S. Review of The Star Road. Luna Monthly [fanzine],
        no. 54 (September):22.
                An uneven collection: Dickson can write well, "but far
        too often he strings together a series of dismal clichés."

D138   MOSLANDER, C. Review of Alien Art. Luna Monthly [fanzine],
        no. 53 (August):16.
                Appreciates the different levels: conflict between
        colonists and Earth; attempts to understand nonhuman intel-
        ligence; an adventure tale.

*D139   OZANNE, K. Review of Sleepwalker's World. Son of WSFA Journal
        [fanzine], no. 121 (January):5.
                [Source: Hall, SFBRI 5 (1974):11.]

D140   RUSS, JOANNA. "Books." FSF 46 (February):71-72.
                Review of The Star Road: Enjoys "the usual interesting
        and varied Dickson aliens," and considers that in "Building
        on the Line," he "writes magnificently of the psychology of
        stress and delirium, little as I like his politics."

D141   TUCK, DONALD H. "Dickson, Gordon R(upert)." In The
        Encyclopedia of Science Fiction and Fantasy through 1968.
        Vol. 1, Who's Who, A-L. Chicago: Advent, p. 143.
                Brief biographical outline, followed by listing of novels
        with two-line comments.

D142   WALKER, P. Review of The R-Master. Luna Monthly [fanzine],
        no. 52 (May):17.
                A sweeping, subjective condemnation: plots labored,
        prose and ideas uninspired, characters two-dimensional.

                                1975

D143   ANON. Review of Ancient, My Enemy. LJ 71 (15 February):611.
                An appealing collection, marked by "humor, poignancy,
        romance, adventure."

D144   ANON. Review of Combat SF. KR 43 (15 April):480.
                These stories of destruction in the future are "just
        fair."

D145   ANON. Review of Soldier, Ask Not. PW, 13 October, p. 113.
                This expansion of the novelette "retains the virtue of
        concentration on story line while enriching characterization
        and background." Praises the "unusually effective blend of
        idea and action."

D146   BODART, JONI. Review of Combat SF. School Library Journal 22
        (November):95.

These stories are "angry, frightening, and thought provoking."

D147 BRODSKY, ALLYN B. Review of The R-Master. Science Fiction Review Monthly, no. 1 (March):20.
The action is swift, the book interesting; but the "breadth of concept is less than Dickson's best," and the hero grows irritating.

D148 BROWN, C. Review of Combat SF and The R-Master. Locus [fanzine], 3 June, p. 5.
Comments only upon the "awful" cover of the former; the latter is a "minor adventure novel," competent but uninspiring.

D149 _____. Review of Sleepwalker's World. Locus [fanzine], 27 October, p. 5.
Considers the author has written much better than this "mildly interesting intrigue novel."

D150 BURK, J. Review of Combat SF. Delap's F&SF Review 1 (August): 13-14.
This anthology is "smooth and balanced," with wide appeal.

*D151 BURNS, S. Review of The Star Road. WSFA Journal [fanzine] 85 (August):R23.
[Source: Hall, SFBRI 6 (1975):13.]

D152 CONAN, NEAL J. Review of Combat SF. Science Fiction Review Monthly, no. 6 (August):9.
Finds only four good stories in this "generally undistinguished" anthology.

D153 DALMYN, TONY. "The Prince among the Planets: Machiavelli and Gordon Dickson." Winding Numbers [fanzine] 1 (Fall):5-7.
Argues, convincingly as far as he goes, that "Dickson demonstrates a theory similar to that of Machiavelli" in certain novels where the hero perceives and acts to influence the pattern of power relationships in interstellar politics.

D154 GINSBURG, R. Review of The R-Master. Kliatt Paperback Book Guide 9 (April):84.
A "rich exciting story of intrigue . . . that keeps the reader guessing constantly."

D155 JONAS, GERALD. "Of Things to Come." New York Times Book Review, 14 September, pp. 22, 26.
Review of Combat SF: Complains that the general level of writing is bad.

D156 MacPHERSON, W.N. Review of <u>Soldier, Ask Not</u>. <u>Science Fiction</u>
<u>Review Monthly</u>, no. 9 (November):18.
Complains that the reader cannot identify with the protagonist, who is "most singularly unattractive and egocen-
tric." This, together with "the comic book morality, simplistic Darwinian philosophy, and suspect verisimilitude
seriously damage this novel." Inferior to other Dorsai
books.

D157 MILLER, DAN. Review of <u>Combat SF</u>. <u>Booklist</u> 72 (1 September):
28.
"Stories generally concentrate on the brutalizing effect
of combat on individuals and the heroism it can coax from
the unwilling. . . . A superior collection of its kind."

D158 ROBINSON, SPIDER. "Galaxy Bookshelf." <u>Galaxy</u> 36 (September):
137-38.
Review of <u>Combat SF</u>: Recommends this "excellent representative selection . . . without reservation."

D159 _____. "Galaxy Bookshelf." <u>Galaxy</u> 36 (August):150-51.
Review of <u>The R-Master</u>: Finds some of the characterization "sketchy," some questions left unanswered, and the
ending unsatisfying; but the story is action-packed and
thought-provoking.

D160 WALKER, P. Review of <u>Ancient, My Enemy</u>. <u>Luna Monthly</u>
[fanzine], no. 57 (Spring):13.
Dismisses this "badly written" collection as "forgetable."

D161 WEINER, PAULA J. Review of Combat SF. LJ 100 (1 June):1155-56.
These tales "display widely ranging styles and attitudes,"
though they can become monotonous if read all together.

*D162 WOOSTER, M. Review of <u>Combat SF</u>. <u>WSFA Journal</u> [fanzine], no.
85 (August):R20-R21.
[Source: Hall, <u>SFBRI</u> 6 (1975):13.]

1976

D163 ANON. Review of <u>The Dragon and the George</u>. <u>PW</u>, 6 September,
p. 66.
Praises the story as "good fun."

D164 ANON. Review of <u>The Lifeship</u>. <u>KR</u> 44 (1 April):425.
"No surprises here--just intelligent SF."

D165 ANON. Review of <u>The Lifeship</u>. <u>PW</u>, 5 April, p. 101.
Combines "wry speculation on class prejudice with exciting space opera."

Part D: Critical Studies

D166   ANON. Review of Naked to the Stars. PW, 6 December, p. 61.
        Didactic intent meshes smoothly with good action and
        character portrayal.

D167   ANON. Review of "The Mortal and the Monster." PW, 6 September,
        p. 66.
        A compelling story that "combines emotional force with
        a portrait of a believable nonhuman."

D168   BADAMI, MARY KENNY. "A Feminist Critique of Science Fiction."
        Extrapolation 18 (December):6-19.
        Includes a brief criticism of the Childe Cycle for treat-
        ing women as property and the spoils of war (pp. 8-9).

D169   BIRLEM, LYNNE M. Review of The Lifeship. School Library
        Journal 23 (December):74.
        The action is slowed by "ponderous and intrusive discus-
        sions about honor, duty, control."

D170   CROSS, MICHAEL S. Review of The Lifeship. LJ 101 (July):1557.
        While not up to the best of either Dickson or Harrison,
        the plot is "gripping," the science interesting, and the
        hero a "well realized character in a thoughtful story."

D171   D'AMMASSA, DON. Review of Ancient, My Enemy. SF Booklog, no.
        9 (May-June):7.
        Comments upon each story, then concludes that although
        none of Dickson's best known appear it is "a collection of
        very competent stories, light entertainments, but with ac-
        curate and thoughtful depictions of human endeavors."

D172   DAVIS, MONTE. Review of Spacepaw. Science Fiction Review
        Monthly, no. 16 (June):12-13.
        Casually and sardonically dismisses the novel for its
        tediously improbable plot and obtuse characters.

D173   del REY, LESTER. "The Reference Library." ASF 96 (May):169.
        Review of Dorsai! Hails the novel as "a classic . . .
        that really established Dickson as a major writer."

D174   _____. "The Reference Library." ASF 96 (February):172-73.
        Review of Three to Dorsai! Finds Necromancer weakest of
        the three; this collection in one volume is "useful."

D175   GEIS, RICHARD E. "Short, Pithy Reviews by Reg." Science
        Fiction Review [fanzine], no. 18 (August):31.
        Review of The Lifeship: A "gripping space adventure"
        that sinks into "idealistic incredibility at the end."

*D176   GOLDFRANK, J. Review of The Dragon and the George. SF & F
        Newsletter [fanzine], no. 13 (October):3.
        [Source: Hall, SFBRI 7 (1976):15.]

Part D: Critical Studies

D177   JONAS, GERALD. "For Young Readers: Science Fiction." New
        York Times Book Review, 25 January, p. 12.
                Review of Star Prince Charlie: Considers this an enjoy-
        able parody of the clichés in science fiction, provided that
        the reader is familiar enough with the field not to mistake
        the story as "silly."

D178   JUSTICE, K. Review of The Lifeship. SF Booklog, no. 11
        (September-October):8.
                Story is good, "ordinary craftsmanlike work," but ulti-
        mately unconvincing; and the characters seem to be manipu-
        lated.

D179   LIVINGSTONE, DENNIS. "Science Fiction Survey." Futures 8
        (August):361.
                Review of The Lifeship: Praises the story as "rich both
        on the characterisation level and on the conceptual level;
        at the end it holds open the possibility of mutual respect
        between individualistic humans and fatalistic aliens--and
        between humans and humans."

D180   McGUIRE, PAUL. "Yes, but How Much Do They Weigh?" Science
        Fiction Review [fanzine], no. 18 (August):25.
                Review of Gremlins, Go Home! The hero grows in maturity
        in a "tongue-in-cheek," fast-paced adventure that is "opti-
        mistic, unpretentious fun."

D181   McMURRAY, C. Review of Ancient, My Enemy. Delap's F&SF Review
        2 (October):28.
                Contains a surprising number of "mediocre and downright
        bad stories."

D182   _____. Review of Soldier, Ask Not. Delap's F&SF Review 2
        (March):23-24.
                Finds that additions diminish the dramatic impact of the
        earlier novelette.

D183   _____. Review of Three to Dorsai! Delap's F&SF Review 2
        (March):9-11.
                Dorsai! shows flashes of brilliance, but "suffers from
        rough notes". Necromancer is saved from dullness by the
        "rich texture" of the writing, but suffers from structural
        problems and the obtrusiveness of philosophical material
        important to the series. The Tactics of Mistake is best in
        series to date.

D184   MacPHERSON, W.N. Review of Dorsai! Science Fiction Review
        Monthly, no. 12 (February):10.
                Review of Dorsai! After comments upon the protagonist's
        search for maturity, complains of similarities to Van Vogt,
        "muddled philosophy," and lack of impact and realism.

D185   MEACHAM, BETH, and KING, TAPPAN. Review of The Lifeship.
        Science Fiction Review Monthly, no. 16 (June):17.
              The aliens possess a "rich strangeness"; otherwise the
        "work is slightly mechanical in terms of plot and character,
        but it moves tautly and swiftly."

D186   _____. Review of Star Prince Charlie. Science Fiction Review
        Monthly, no. 16 (June):16-17.
              Highly recommends this novel, which combines "broad farce
        ＼ith the insightful tale of a youth's maturing," and which
        walks "a narrow line between the absurd and the dramatic."

D187   MILLER, DAN. Review of The Lifeship. Booklist 73 (1 September):
        23.
              Praises this "exciting adventure" story.

D188   _____. Review of The Lifeship. Chicago Daily News Panorama,
        22 May, p. 8. Reprint. 26 June, p. 11.
              "Intrigue, double-cross, friendship and dignity surface
        in this exciting, ofttimes melodramatic novel."

D189   MINES, S. Review of Combat SF. Luna Monthly [fanzine], no.
        66 (Winter):42.
              Considers this an uneven, but "fairly interesting" an-
        thology; complains that some tales are "slow-moving."

D190   PATTEN, F. Review of The Dragon and the George. Delap's F&SF
        Review 2 (December):23.
              Enjoyable, but minor work; the plot is drawn-out, "but
        the characters are likeable enough to carry the reader
        through to the end."

D191   _____. Review of Spacepaw. Delap's F&SF Review 2 (September):
        24.
              "Fast-moving fun," though dated by derivation from Cold
        War politics and Peace Corps diplomacy.

D192   _____. Review of Star Prince Charlie. Delap's F&SF Review 2
        (June):21-22.
              Enjoys the "light humor," but believes the novel lacks
        depth, despite a tendency to moralize occasionally.

D193   SANDERS, J. Review of The Lifeship. Delap's F&SF Review 2
        (September):6-7.
              Considers the novel to be quite smoothly executed, but
        "crushingly mediocre" and predictable, despite some inter-
        esting elements.

D194   SHIRK, JIM. Review of Ancient, My Enemy. Science Fiction
        Review Monthly, no. 15 (May):21.
              Perceives these stories as "a celebration of the somber

joys of conflict between man and alien, between man and the
Universe, or between man and man," paralleled by internal
conflict as the hero struggles to overcome his weaknesses.
Grumbles that "to get along in the Dicksonian Universe requires a strong will."

D195   SLATER, I. Review of The Dragon and the George. Fantasiae
       [fanzine] 4 (October):6-7.
          Praises "fast-moving, very humorous" action. "Charac-
       terization is fairly heavy-handed . . . but this fits the
       rather broad slapstick humour, and the rather elementary
       (although not obtrusive) moral lessons learned by a number
       of major characters."

D196   WIXON, DAVE. Review of Dorsai! SF Booklog, no. 10 (July-
       August):8.
          Considers the hero a superb creation: "As should be ex-
       pected, we humans cannot totally penetrate the differentness
       of Donal--but we can feel his presence, his reality, the
       force of his driving personality." Moreover, he helps us
       to "see in depth the society Dickson envisions."

D197   WOOSTER, MARTIN. Review of The Dragon and the George. SF
       Booklog, no. 11 (September-October):4.
          Approves of the author's success in involving the reader
       in the action and the many "hilarious scenes." The novel
       "has it all--interesting characters, convincing dialogue,
       magic, and lots of battles in an action-packed enjoyable
       adventure."

*D198 _____. Review of Star Prince Charlie. SF Booklog, no. 9
       (May-June):6.
          [Source: Hall, SFBRI 7 (1976):5.]

                              1977

D199   ANON. Review of Time Storm. KR 45 (1 September):955.
          "Real concern here is tense, hard-driven Marc's gradual,
       portentous transformation through the bonds of love and
       trust he forges with his fellow-survivors. Dickson can
       create interesting situations and likable individuals," but
       buries them under "a lot of pseudo-scientific props and a
       graceless prolixity."

D200   ANON. Review of Time Storm. PW, 5 September, p. 68.
          Concepts are handled with masterful "clarity and inter-
       est."

D201   A., R.G. Review of The Dragon and the George. Kliatt Paperback
       Book Guide 11 (Spring):10.

Finds the book "just plain fun," the action "fast-paced and sure to be a hit."

D202 BUDRYS, ALGIS. "Books." FSF 52 (April):35-37.
Review of The Dragon and the George: Praises this "marvellous fantasy": "Eckart and Gorbash grow up on this journey from post-adolescence to primacy; we remember a little of what is good in us from travelling with them . . . resembles real life as only the best fantasy can."

D203 CARPER, STEVE. Review of The Pritcher Mass. Delap's F&SF Review 2 (February):33.
Complains at this "ground-out quickie," with its incoherent plot, stock characters, and simplistic morality.

D204 CLUTE, JOHN. "Books." FSF 52 (February):49-51.
Review of The Lifeship: The model of trapping a group of interesting characters in a lifeboat has potential, but seems contrived. The story is limited by confusion and coincidence: below standard for both Dickson and Harrison.

D205 JONAS, GERALD. "Science Fiction." New York Times Book Review, 25 December, p. 11.
Review of Time Storm: Starts very well, as the characters move against "a background built up of precisely observed detail"; but in the second part the "sense of reality begins to seep out of the story," as "too many marvels deflect and, ultimately, deaden the reader's sense of wonder."

D206 MILLER, DAN. Review of The Dragon and the George. Booklist 73 (1 March):994.
Admires the author's firm control of "this zesty fantasy, never allowing it to degenerate into farce or insipid burlesque."

1978

D207 ANON. Review of The Far Call. KR 46 (15 January):67.
Grumbles that here are "the makings of a strong cautionary comment on space-exploration programs . . . but somehow the makings never get properly assembled."

D208 ANON. Review of The Far Call. PW, 6 March, p. 89.
Complains about the "excessive number of diversions" in the story.

D209 ANON. Review of Time Storm. Virginia Quarterly Review 54 (Spring):66.
Observes that in seeking civilization, the characters "discover themselves": a "strange book."

D210   A., R.G. Review of Alien Art. Kliatt Paperback Book Guide
       12 (Fall):17.
             "A simple, fast-moving story with pointed commentary on
       technological, artistic, religious and biological chauvin-
       ism." Morality is "rather simplistic."

D211   BROWN, CHARLES N. "On Books." Isaac Asimov's Science Fiction
       Magazine 2 (September–October):16.
             Review of The Far Call: Decides that "space scenes and
       the picture of the space program are realistic and impres-
       sive, while the political infighting furnishes the melo-
       drama," but that the novel is a "bit too long."

D212   _____. "On Books." Isaac Asimov's Science Fiction Magazine 2
       (March–April):15.
             Review of Time Storm: "Dickson's best book to date. It
       has a level of sympathetic characterization and a smoothness
       of style he has never reached before." The plot is "pretty
       exciting" despite "a tendency to stretch out the middle sec-
       tion."

D213   del REY, LESTER. "The Reference Library." ASF 98 (January):
       171.
             Review of Time Storm: First part is a "good adventure
       story with a lot of inventive angles"; the second shows man
       against the universe. Some of the characters are "fascinat-
       ing" and "complicated . . . but the real interest is nearly
       always focused by those characters, as it should be."

D214   _____. "The Reference Library." ASF 98 (May):171.
             Review of The Far Call: Revisions to the original serial
       make the story "much deeper and more convincing." The em-
       phasis on character is stronger, and the political struggles
       in the subplots "relate to and deepen the main point of the
       story." Judges it "the most mature of all Dickson's novels."

D215   EVANS, CHRIS. Review of None but Man. Vector [fanzine], no.
       86 (March–April):38.
             Condemns the opening chapters for the "ominous predicta-
       bility" of quickly written work; the characters as "peculiar-
       ly colourless"; and Dickson for squandering his talents on
       "tedious effusions such as this."

D216   FRENKEL, JAMES R. Foreword to Gordon R. Dickson's SF Best.
       New York: Dell, pp. 11–12.
             In describing his task as editor, pays tribute to the
       "experimental nature" of Dickson's writing that contributes
       to its excellence.

D217   _____. "Gordon R. Dickson Bibliography." In Gordon R.
       Dickson's SF Best. New York: Dell, pp. 223–36.
             This listing is incomplete and the data limited.

D218   GEIS, RICHARD E. Review of Time Storm. Science Fiction Review
        [fanzine], no. 24 (February):15.
            Sharply criticizes the novel as "a dishonest crock, epi-
        sodic, and carelessly written." The first part is "episodic
        with slow spots of busywork, less and less tension"; in the
        second part, the universe is saved with ridiculous ease.

D219   GILLESPIE, J. "New Novel May Be Dickson's Best." Minneapolis
        Tribune, 1 January, p. 15D.
            Review of Time Storm: Appreciates the careful balance
        between the hero's external struggle to control the time
        storm and his internal realization of sterile emptiness,
        which leads to acceptance and growth.

D220   KEMSKE, FLOYD. Review of Time Storm. Galileo 7 (March):89.
            Sees the novel as "a tour-de-force of sf characteriza-
        tion": the hero's development of ability to deal with the
        time storm is "integral to the growth of his powers of self-
        realization." Complains, however, of the confusing explana-
        tion for the time storm phenomenon.

D221   KVAM, BRUCE. "Ad Astra!" Minnesota Technolog 59 (Fall II):
        10-11.
            Very general appreciation of the realism, both techno-
        logical and political, in Dickson's novels. [Note: See
        also entry C51.]

D222   MIESEL, SANDRA. "About Gordon R. Dickson." In Alien Art.
        New York: Dutton, 1973, pp. 163-66. Reprint. In Arcturus
        Landing. New York: Ace, pp. 214-17. *Rev. ed. "Biograph-
        ical Sketch of Gordon R. Dickson." Okon '80 Program Book,
        July 1980. [Source: photocopy of author's manuscript.]
            Succinctly outlines the range of Dickson's achievements,
        commenting briefly upon biography, literary theory and
        craftsmanship, the Childe Cycle, the Hokas, and animals in
        his writings.

D223   _____. Afterword to Home from the Shore. New York: Sunridge
        Press, pp. 207-21.
            Perceptive study of Home from the Shore and The Space
        Swimmers, showing how Dickson explores the problems of human
        survival and growth through the conflict between the uncon-
        scious/conservative and the conscious/progressive sides of
        human nature: "Dickson expresses his theme of polarities
        uniting by setting pairs of groups, characters, phenomena,
        ideas, and images in parallel and recording their interac-
        tions."

D224   MILLER, DAN. Review of Nebula Winners Twelve. Booklist 74
        (1 February):897.
            Praises this anthology as "a superior collection of

provocative and mature sf" with "a decidedly philosophical
bent."

D225   _____. Review of Time Storm. Booklist 74 (1 February):895.
             Praises the "sturdily drawn characters, exciting action,
        and a thoughtful plot--in one of the notable science fiction
        novels of the year."

*D226   NEWMAN, C. Review of Alien Art. Voice of Youth Advocates 1
        (October):37.
             [Source: Hall, SFBRI 9 (1978):10.]

D227   ROBINSON, SPIDER. "Introduction: The Quiet Giant." In
        Gordon R. Dickson's SF Best. New York: Dell, pp. 7-10.
             Warmly praises Dickson's unobtrusive excellence as a
        writer and his helpful and genial nature as a human being.

D228   SMITH, BARBARA J. Review of Nebula Winners Twelve. LJ 103
        (15 May):1086.
             "Except for the overwritten introduction and two gratui-
        tous essays on literary criticism, this is a fine book."

D229   WALKER, P. "Galaxy Bookshelf." Galaxy 39 (April):157-58.
             Review of Time Storm: Considers that the story operates
        on three levels: the struggle of postholocaust survivors;
        the problem of the time storm; the spiritual pilgrimage to
        self-discovery. The hero's soul-searching grows boring, but
        the complicated plot is well handled to create an exciting,
        if superficial, story.

D230   _____. "Galaxy Bookshelf." Galaxy 39 (May):135-38.
             Review of The Far Call: Praises the novel for its "mas-
        terful" use of character. "The pace is slow, but the sus-
        pense is cumulative." It represents "the best sf has to
        offer to literature, the ability to make us live the future
        today and to understand that the future is as much a part of
        today as is the past."

D231   _____. "Galaxy Bookshelf." Galaxy 39 (November-December):
        136-39.
             Review of Nebula Winners Twelve: Approves "some excellent
        choices," and finds Dickson's introduction "intelligent and
        interesting, if typical of these anthologies." However,
        disputes not only Dickson's contention that science fiction
        is indefinable, but also some critical statements in the
        two essays in the anthology.

                              1979

D232   ANON. "Paperbacks: New & Noteworthy." New York Times Book

                              69

<u>Review</u>, 28 January, p. 37.

Review of <u>Time Storm</u>: Praises this "precisely observed picture of three survivors wandering across the face of an eerie America," but regrets that Dickson's "wonders never cease, ultimately deadening his reader's sense of marvel."

D233 BROWN, CHARLES N. "On Books." <u>Isaac Asimov's Science Fiction Magazine</u> 3 (March):14.

Review of <u>Home from the Shore</u> and <u>Pro</u>: Finds that the former, which details a "clash between cultures, is high-quality Dickson . . . a solid adventure story," but that the latter "seems padded."

D234 BUDRYS, ALGIS. Review of <u>Pro</u>. <u>Booklist</u> 75 (1 February):856.

Praises the novel as a "fast-moving" adventure tale.

D235 LAMBE, DEAN R. Review of <u>The Spirit of Dorsai</u> and <u>Home from the Shore</u>. <u>Science Fiction and Fantasy Book Review</u> 1 (November):137.

Recommends the former for "some of the best writing in the field" of behavioral genetics, but is unenthusiastic about the latter.

D236 McMURRAY, CLIFFORD. "The Different Man: Dickson's Donal Graeme." <u>The Diversifier</u> [fanzine], no. 5 (February-March): 27-32, 60.

A close analysis of <u>Dorsai!</u> that focuses upon the "fascinating portrait of Donal Graeme's growth from a remarkable human being into a figure of supra-human dimensions." Notes both similarities and differences between Donal and his principal antagonist. Contains sound observations whose implications are not followed up fully.

D237 _____. Review of <u>Gordon R. Dickson's SF Best</u>. <u>Science Fiction Review</u> [fanzine] 30 (March-April):54-55.

Considers the bibliography inadequate, and, with some exceptions, the choice poor; but praises the tales for their "consummate craftsmanship" and range, from humor to deepest tragedy.

D238 MIESEL, SANDRA. Review of <u>The Far Call</u>. <u>Science Fiction Review</u> [fanzine] 29 (January-February):43.

Hails this as "Dickson's most ambitious and most satisfying single novel to date," in which he "weaves a host of multiple viewpoints together" smoothly. Finds the setting "authentic" and the characters "believable," and praises the "significant advance" in the author's handling of female characters.

D239 O'REILLY, TIMOTHY. "The Childe Cycle." In <u>Survey of Science Fiction Literature</u>. Vol. 1. Edited by Frank N. Magill.

Englewood Cliffs, N.J.: Salem Press, pp. 330-36.
A thoughtful study of the first four novels of the Cycle and those that have been projected. Sees Dickson as "the master of the superhero story," though suggests that "the weakness of these heroes is their lack of introspection." All the books are about the evolution of "responsible man,"; the "distinctive quality of the Childe Cycle rests in its portrayal of a species-wide response to the evolutionary challenge" by dividing into "splinter cultures," each "embodying a different facet of human personality." These will eventually be reunited. Proceeds to show how each novel fits into this conceptual framework, and ponders future direction.

D240   THOMPSON, RAYMOND H. "Shai Dorsai! A Study of the Hero Figure in Gordon R. Dickson's Dorsai!" Extrapolation 20 (Fall): 223-29.
Uses Dorsai! to argue that Dickson writes in the romance mode, where the hero figure serves to explore ideals of human behavior. Donal exhibits not only various heroic virtues, notably a strong sense of duty, but also the human cost of asserting these virtues. He is responsible for the death of his brother, but recognition of guilt becomes a vital step in his growth to the full self-awareness necessary for the truly responsible man. [Note: First appearance of a critical article on Dickson in an academic journal.]

D241   WOOD, EDWARD. "The Reference Library." ASF 99 (August):172.
Review of Pro: Judges that the ambitious protagonist is limited by lack of compassion; complains that the author "manipulates" his characters in "much too convenient a fashion."

1980

D242   EASTON, TOM. "The Reference Library." ASF 100 (March):167-68.
Review of Home from the Shore and The Spirit of Dorsai: Considers the former "moving enough, though told in a flat, simple style," and a pleasure to read. The novelettes in the latter "throw interesting light on the Dorsai people, and are both worth reading in their own rights."

D243   GREEN, ROLAND. Review of In Iron Years. Booklist 77 (15 September):99.
Praises the "exceptional precision and clarity of Dickson's prose" in this "admirably worthwhile" collection.

D244   _____. Review of Lost Dorsai. Booklist 77 (15 October):308.
Considers the title novel "well-crafted"; "Warrior" a

"quietly chilling portrait of Ian Graeme, the man of war"; Miesel's essay is "warmly enthusiastic and highly informative."

D245   _____. Review of The Spirit of Dorsai. Booklist 76 (February):760.
      Considers "Brothers" a "powerful" story; "Amanda Morgan" "contains some of the finest writing Dickson has ever done, and the heroine is arguably his best piece of characterization and one of the half dozen best female characters in sf or fantasy during the last decade."

D246   HERBERT, ROSEMARY. Review of In Iron Years. LJ 105 (August): 1664.
      Praises this "powerful anthology," which "well represents the varied talents of this author whose works are always interesting and imaginative."

D247   KLEIN, JAY KAY. "Biolog: Gordon R. Dickson." ASF 100 (August):39.
      Brief biographical outline.

D248   _____. "The Dorsai Irregulars." Destinies 1 (February):132-33.
      Describes a paramilitary group, inspired by Dickson's Dorsai series, that performs security duty at science fiction conventions.

D249   MIESEL, SANDRA. "The Plume and the Sword." Destinies 2 (February–March):116-31. Rev. ed. In Lost Dorsai, New York: Ace.
      A perceptive and appreciative general assessment of Dickson as a person and as a writer, followed by an explanation of the plan of the Childe Cycle. The revised version adds a literary appreciation of the various short stories ("Illuminations"), which augment the novels of the Cycle. Notes particularly the importance of balance ("the harmony of opposites") in the overall pattern of the Cycle and in the individual tales: "Each illumination examines the twin moral issues of integrity and responsibility: how can human beings reconcile what they must be with what they must do?" [Note: Revised version omits the opening section, describing how author's interest in Dickson grew, and adds ten pages of critical analysis.]

D250   _____. Review of The Spirit of Dorsai. Science Fiction Review [fanzine], no. 35 (May):31-32.
      Judges that "balancing 'Amanda Morgan' against 'Brothers' allows Dickson to demonstrate the martial spirit of Dorsai operating at home and abroad." Praises female characterization in the former, where the heroine is "a wonderfully convincing blend of courage and vulnerability, competence and

anxiety". "Brothers" explores "the corrosiveness of self-hatred, the horror of brother-slaying, the hero's saving death."

D251   _____. "The Road to the Dark Tower." In <u>Dorsai!</u> New York: Ace, pp. 273-305. [Note: See entry A96.]
An extended and wide-ranging examination of the Childe Cycle, particularly valuable for the information provided on the projected novels that remain to be written. Comments extensively upon mythical motifs in Dickson's work and contends that the cycle fits the theories of mythologist George Dumezil. Analyses the relationship between the "three major Splinter Cultures--Spirit, Mind, and Body" (Friendlies, Exotics, and Dorsai); all are destined to be reintegrated as the human race moves through "the initiatory pattern of separation-perfection-reunion." Comments interestingly upon the developing role of women in the cycle.

D252   SEARLES, BAIRD. "On Books." <u>Isaac Asimov's Science Fiction Magazine</u> 4 (January):16.
Review of <u>The Spirit of Dorsai</u>: Suggests that "Dorsai devotees" will find the two novelettes "fascinating footnotes to the Dorsai epic, but it will seem pretty mysterious to non-initiates."

D253   _____. "On Books." <u>Isaac Asimov's Science Fiction Magazine</u> 4 (March):15.
Review of <u>Earthman's Burden</u>: Praises the collection as "one of science fiction's rare excursions into palatable humor"; the results of the Hoka's imitations are "predictably chaotic."

D254   THOMPSON, RAYMOND H. "Gordon R. Dickson: Science Fiction for Young Canadians." <u>Canadian Children's Literature</u>, nos. 15-16 [Summer]:38-46.
Argues that traces of Dickson's Canadian background appear in his fiction, including the conflict between the individual and the "garrison mentality"; that all his novels have special appeal to adolescents because they show young heroes succeeding where their elders fail; and that they have special value for young people since they are about growing up, learning to accept responsibility.

Appendixes

A: Overview of MSS 39, The Gordon R. Dickson Papers, Manuscript Division, University of Minnesota Libraries

The Gordon R. Dickson papers are collected in an archive that presently consists of eighty-five boxes. Material is steadily being added, resulting in an ongoing process of revision. The archive contains outlines, handwritten and typed notes, rough and final drafts, foundry proofs, and final galleys for poems, plays, and fiction that ranges from papers for creative writing classes during Dickson's university days; to short stories, both published and unpublished; to novels and collections of short stories. Many of the early pieces are non-science fiction.

The following is an overview of the Gordon R. Dickson papers at the University of Minnesota Libraries--MSS 39. Since the task of sorting the papers and compiling the inventory is still incomplete, it would be misleading to give a precise description of the holdings dealt with so far. Hence I am providing only a list of the works now represented in the collection, together with dates where given and identification so far made with entries in the bibliography. Specific and updated details of the extent of the material may be obtained from the curator of the Manuscript Division, Alan K. Lathrop, for whose assistance I am much indebted.

1. SHORT STORIES

"Accident," n.d.
"Act of Creation," 2 May 1955. [A68]
"All for the Love of Ellen," n.d.
"All the Time in the World" ("Nerves"; "A Question of Price"), n.d.
"Allarin," 14 Nov. 1957.
"Amateur Psychology," n.d.
"The Amateurs," 30 Mar. 1959. [A117]
"The Amulet," n.d. [A93]

"An Honorable Death," n.d. [A115]
"And in a Strange Land," 18 May 1954.
"And Then There Was Peace," 6 Jan. 1962. [A131]
"The Army .45," 7 Jan. 1956.
"Aunty's Got a Gun," n.d.
"Babes in the Wood," n.d. [A24]
"The Beast Men of Snupifon," n.d.
"The Best of It," n.d.
"The Best Reason," n.d.
"Black Charlie," 1953-54. [A35]

Appendix A

"The Black One and the Grey,"
  n.d.
"The Black Panther," 30 October
  1951.
"The Bleak and Barren Land,"
  22 November 1951. [A23]
"The Blessed," 3 February 1959.
"Blood Call to Broken Bow,"
  24 July 1951.
"The Breaking of Jerry McCloud,"
  n.d. [A30]
"Breakthrough Gang," n.d. [A156]
"Brother Charlie," 8 January
  1958. [A84]
"Bunny Goes for Chinese," n.d.
"Button, Button," July 1959.
  [A109]
"By New Hearth Fires" ("One
  Friend Have I"), 19 March
  1958. [A90]
"Call Him Lord," 26 July 1965.
  [A158]
"Cancel" ("Mx Knows Best"),
  7 March 1956. [A70]
"The Canteen," n.d.
"Cap'n Flint," n.d.
"Carry Me Home," n.d. [A40]
"A Case History," 24 January
  1953. [A42]
"The Case of the Case to End All
  Cases," n.d.
"The Catch," 23 April 1958. [A94]
"Catch a Tartar," n.d. [A150]
"The Cautious Heart," 11 July
  1954.
"The Christmas Present," 19 April
  1957. [A79]
"The Clay God," 24 November 1958.
"Cloak and Stagger," 29 November
  1954. [A71]
"Cloth of Red," n.d.
"The Clumsy Cadaver Case" ("The
  Case of the Clumsy Cadaver"),
  n.d. [A108]
"Communications" ("Tiger
  Green"), n.d. [A155]
"Computers Don't Argue," April
  1965. [A151]
"The Comrades," 20 November 1956.
  [Note: Contemporary tale,
  elements of which were later

used in Dorsai! (A96) and
  Naked to the Stars (A123).]
"The Cruel Lion-Trainer," n.d.
"Cry, Bones," 22 February 1956.
"Danger--Human!" 25 February
  1957. [A77]
"Death, and the Living" ("Home-
  coming"), 17 February 1958.
  [A98]
"Different Laws," n.d.
"The Dog Killers," 15 August 1961.
"Dolphin's Way," n.d. [A142]
"Don't Be Mean to Little Kids,"
  n.d.
"The Duty of Ian Graeme" (draft
  of what became "Warrior"),
  n.d. [A157]
"E Gubling Dow," n.d. [A97]
"Eight Days," n.d.
"Emotional Factor," March 1965.
"Eppur Si Muove!" n.d.
"Evolution," 28 October 1952.
"The Faithful Nard," 26 November
  1957.
"The Faithful Wilf," n.d. [A139]
"The Ferret," n.d.
"FIDO," 3 May 1957. [A75]
"Final Contact" ("Flat Tiger"),
  n.d. [A57]
"First Fall," n.d.
"5Q 1 5Q," 30 January 1957.
"For the Old Man is Very Cunning,"
  n.d.
"For Old Time's Sake," 20 November
  1957.
"A Fragment and a Song," n.d.
"Friday at Alvin's," n.d.
"Future for Demons," 26 March 1955.
"The Galloping Salamanders,"
  24 September 1952.
"The Game of Five," n.d. [A103]
"The General and the Axe,"
  16 December 1956. [A76]
"The Gentle Heart," 12 December
  1951.
"The Gentlemen from Ihmritar,"
  n.d.
"Gifts," 14 December 1957. [A88]
"Grampa Likes You," 11 March 1957.
"Graveyard," 6 January 1953. [A27]
"The Greatest Punchline Ever Told,"

"The Green Building," 23 February
1956. [A59]

"The Grim Taste of Success," n.d.

"Guardian Angel," n.d.

"Hand for Lend," n.d.

"Harp Song," n.d.

"The Haunted Village," December
1957. [A121]

"Heaven Has Wheels," n.d.

"Hell Is Redrock County,"
6 August 1951.

"Hilifter," n.d. [A136]

"The Hole in the Mountains,"
13 June 1956. ("The Quitter"),
n.d.

"Homecoming," 7 June 1957. [A98]

"The Hours Are Good," 30 July
1959 [A110]

"How Much Do You Understand?" ca.
1947.

"The Hungry Guns," n.d.

"A Husband for Molly Darlin',"
10 January 1957.

"The Hypothalamic Glasses,"
31 January 1958.

"I Believe You," n.d.

"The Immortal," n.d. [A149]

"Imp's Day Off," 3 July 1958.

"In Iron Years." [A199]

"In the Bone," n.d. [A159]

"Intertime Incident" ("Time
Grabber"), n.d. [A21]

"It Hardly Seems Fair," 29 June
1959. [A104]

"Itco's Strong Right Arm,"
13 August 1951. [A38]

"Jackal's Meal," August 1968.
[A170]

"James," 6 June 1954. [A46]

"Jean Duprès," n.d. [A179]

"Joe and the Declining Years,"
28 March 1955.

"John B. Tompkins," 23 October
1956.

"Just Before Noon," n.d.

"A King for Talyina" (<u>Star Prince
Charlie</u>), n.d. [A201]

"The Last Cruise of the
Teakettle" ("Last Voyage"),
6 November 1953. [A85]

"The Last Fire," n.d.

"The Little Tailor," n.d.

"Live a Little," n.d.

"Lorna Fitch," n.d.

"Lost Apronstrings," n.d.

"Love and the Monster," n.d.

"Love Me True," 8 August 1960.
[A122]

"Mad Dog!" 16 August 1951.

"Magic With Words--Example One"
("The Heroic Villain"), n.d.

"Man of Courage," n.d.

"The Man Who Lives in the
Billboard," n.d.

"The Man Who Looked Like Voland"
(earlier version of "The Clay
God"), n.d.

"Manners for the Meekis," n.d.

"The Marshal Is a Lady," 16 June
1954.

"A Matter of Faith," n.d.

"A Matter of Technique," 19 April
1957. [A82]

"A Method of Reconciling Sporadic
Income of the Writer with the
Normal Social System of Regular
Periodic Obligations--Report on
the Use of an Imaginary Bank
Balance," n.d.

"Minotaur," n.d. [A118]

"Miss Prinks" ("Superlady"),
25 August 1952. [A36]

"The Monkey Wrench," n.d. [A11]

"Moon, June, Spoon, Croon,"
14 June 1953. [A47]

"Mr. Willer Does His Bit" ("The
Dreamsman"), 29 July 1957.
[A89]

"Nail and Hammer," n.d.

"Napoleon's Skullcap," 24 February
1960. [A127]

"Natural Enemy" ("The Invaders"),
9 September 1951. [A19]

"Never Too Old" (another version
of "The Blessed"), n.d.

"No More Miracles, Please," n.d.

"Nobody's Mad at Fleegl" ("Fleegl
of Fleegl"), 7 November 1957.
[A81]

"The Obvious," n.d.

"The Odd Ones," 17 November 1953.

[A44]
"Of One Flesh," 12 November 1953.
"Of the People," 19 December
1954. [A53]
"Old Iron," n.d.
"Oliver's Voyage to Lillefout"
("Oliver's Travels"), n.d.
"One on Trial" ("Values"),
27 October 1959. [A106]
"The Only Sons," 3 February 1954.
"Operation P-Button," n.d. [A174]
"Our First Death," 17 December
1954. [A49]
"The Pattern," n.d.
"Pattern for Survival," 26 August
1952.
"Parting Is Not Sweet Sorrow,"
n.d.
"A Picture in Pastels," 3 August
1958.
"Pie a la Mode for Breakfast,"
7 August 1951.
"The Pigeon That Slept on Its
Back" ("Peggy and John"),
21 August 1951.
"The Pikeman," n.d. [Note: Draft
of novel out of which the
Childe Cycle developed; see
entries C17, C30, C55, etc.]
"Planet," n.d.
"Poor Butterfly," n.d.
"Portrait of Martha," 3 April
1954.
"Powerway Emergency." [A186]
"Practice Makes Perfect," n.d.
[A29]
"Prelude to a Blackjack," n.d.
"Press Gang," 24 April 1953.
"Prices," n.d.
"Privacy Right," n.d.
"Psi-Mach," n.d.
"The Quarry," 17 November 1957.
[A87]
"The Queer Critter," 19 March
1953. [A41]
"The Question," 7 June 1957.
[A83]
"The R of A," 15 January 1958.
[A91]
"Ragnarok" ("Just Before the Sun
Goes Down"; "Just at

Twilight," "I've Been Trying
to Tell You"), 19 November
1953. [A99]
"Rapscallion Blood," 12 November
1957.
"The Rebels," 11 October 1951.
[A33]
"Rehabilitated," 23 November 1953.
[A114]
"The Rescue," 16 June 1953. [A37]
"Rescue Mission," 1 April 1956.
[A64]
"Reunion" ("Father of Two"), n.d.
"Rex and Mr. Rejilla," 26 March
1957. [A80]
"Robots Are Nice," 3 March 1957.
[A74]
"Roofs of Silver," ca. 1958.
[A133]
"The Rubber Plant," 22 December
1954.
"To Run and Hide," n.d.
"Run Wild," n.d.
"St. Dragon and the George." [A72]
"Sam" ("Salmanazar"), 2 July 1959.
[A130]
"The Seats of Hell," n.d. [A111]
"Second Best," 14 September 1954.
"The Secret of Success," n.d.
"Seniomsed, Beware!" n.d.
"The Sharp Sparrow," 8 January
1958.
"Show Me the Way to Go Home,"
24 August 1951. [A20]
"Sky," n.d.
"Something Higher," n.d.
"Song of the Meadowlark,"
("Meadowlark's Song"),
6 August 1956.
"Soupstone," 16 April 1964. [A148]
"The Special Angel," 7 March 1956.
"The Star Sworn," n.d.
"Steel Brother," 11 January 1951.
[A14]
"The Storm," n.d.
"Strictly Confidential,"
21 January 1955. [A60]
"Summer's Halfway Over," n.d.
"The Summer Visitors," 17 February
1958. [A105]
"The Swami and the Flack," n.d.

"Take That!" n.d.

"Tempus Non Fugit," 23 March
    1955 to 18 September 1956.
    [A66]

"The Terrible Tyrant of Teol,"
    n.d.

"That's My Advice to You,"
    10 August 1959.

"The Theorist," 8 October 1953.

"The Three," n.d. [A25]

"Timbuctoo," 23 June 1955.

"The Torch," n.d.

"The Tree," 1 April 1956.

"Turn Again, Whittington,"
    24 May 1954. [A67]

"Turnabout," 3 May 1954. [A43]

"The Ultimate Degradation," n.d.

"The Underground" ("The Little
    Captain"), 3 November 1953.
    [A54]

"A Very Clever Game" ("No Shield
    from the Dead"), n.d. [A22]

"Warrior," February 1965 [A157]

"Watch That Worm!" ("The Hard
    Way"), n.d. [A135]

"The Were-Wolfhound" ("The Girl
    Who Played Wolf"), n.d. [A86]

"What Ho, The Enemy!" n.d.

"The White Sheep," n.d.

"Who Dares a Bulbar Eat?"
    ("Greater Love Hath"),
    5 February 1962. [A132]

"Who Screamed?" 5 February 1957.

"Wimin and Johnny Yates,"
    13 November 1953.

"The Wonderful Plastic,"
    14 January 1953.

"A World Named Bartholomew,"
    22 January 1958.

"Zeepsday," 22 February 1956.
    [A58]

"Zero Finds a Friend,"
    17 February 1953.

2. FRAGMENTS (TITLED)

"Adolphus Griggins."

"And All Men Know."

"And Bleed Awhile."

"And the Lord."

"The Art of Angling."

"The Balcony."

"Barin."

"Battle."

"The Baucite Case."

"Before the Snow Flies."

"Behind the Screens."

"Bell Wether."

"The Big Stake."

"The Bodysnatchers."

"The Brothers." [A190]

"Castleman."

"The Check."

"Closing Time."

"Coboy's Fortune." [sic]

"Counter-Irritant." [A31]

"Day of Fire."

"Dear Aunt Jennifer."

"Death Is Easy."

"Death, My Friend."

"Dennis and the Silver Treasure."

"The Devil and Aubrey Dean."

"Don't It [sic] Yourself."

"Early Evening."

"Early in the Morning."

"The Early Train."

"End of the Term."

"The Error of Their Ways."

"Ethics."

"Experimental Error."

"The Fallow Doe."

"Fear."

"Frankie Logan 115 Today."

"Gadget."

"Gal Sal."

"The Game of Five." [A103]

"Gamelyn."

"The Green Bench."

"The Hard Way." [A135]

"Hey, Johnny!" ("Home from the
    Shore"). [A137]

"Hide and Seek."

"Just Before the Sun Goes Down."

"Justice."

"The Knight and the Sword."

"The Last Dream."

"The Lighthouse Keeper" ("Out of
    the Darkness"). [A116]

"Like an Elephant."

"Listen!" [A17]

"Man-X."
"Misplaced."
"The Moment."
"Never Trust a Hoka."
"No More of Earth."
"No One."
"No Provision."
"None Know My Loneliness."
"Number One."
"The Old Wolf."
"One By One."
"The Peace-Wagers."
"Pensioner."
"The Plowman's Tale."
"Prince of a Far Star."
"Project Stupidity."
"The Proud Man."
"Revenge of God."
"Robin Hood of Space."
"Ruthie and the Photographer."
"Sag."
"Samson's Lock."
"The Scholastics."
"The Star Fool." [A13]
"Star Whelp."
"Strange Children."
"Terunaw."
"The Test."
"The Therapeutic Drunk."
"They Call It Christmas."
"Tiger! Tiger!"
"Time vs. Money."
"To Help a Hotzopital."
"The Tummy-Scratchers."
"Two Miles Thick of Ice."
"Unvisible Enemy."
"Waking without Willpower."
"Wanderer."
"Whatever Gods May Be." [A120]
"When the Squigni Came."
"Whipsaw."
"The Worldmakers."
"You, and Who Else?"
"You Don't Have to Be Friends."

3. PHOTOCOPIES OF PUBLISHED
   STORIES

"After the Funeral" [A92]
"The Christmas Present" [A79]

"Computers Don't Argue" [A151]
"The Error of Their Ways" [A10]
"The Haunted Village" [A121]
"Listen" [A17]
"Miss Prinks" [A36]
"The Mousetrap" [A18]
"Of the People" [A53]
"One on Trial" [A106]
"Our First Death" [A49]
"Salmanazar" [A130]
"Three-Part Puzzle" [A129]
"Tiger Green" [A155]
"Warrior" [A157]

4. POETRY

"Assault Soldier's Mourn."
"Autumn."
"Concerning the Future."
"A Cry of Men by Firelight."
"The Enchanted Inn."
"The Enchanted Tower."
"Family Group No. 2."
"H-Bomb Test--1956."
"In Apple Comfort."
"Knight-at-Arms."
"The Last Season."
"Mild Eyes."
"October."
"Pastoral."
"The Pilgrimmage."
"Roundel for Dolores."
"Sickness."
"The Song of Jeffrey Ptolemny."
"A Song of Men."
"Song of Venus."
"S.S. Andrea Doria."
"The Thief."
"Thirty-Seven Years, Five Months,
    Seventeen Days . . ."
"Time."
"Time."
"The Time of the Year."
"To Men with Hoof and Mouth
    Disease."
"Two to Five A.M."
"The Wheel."
Two untitled poems.

5. PLAYS

"Broadsword," July 1962. [Note:
    Outline for a T.V. series.]
"The Decision," 23 April 1958.
    [B8]
"Doom Ship," n.d.
"Don't Call Me Joe," n.d. [See
    note to entry B9.]
"The Gift," 18 March 1958. [B5]
"The Great Gold Bear,"
    30 January 1948. [B3]
"It, Out of Darkest Jungle,"
    2 August 1964. [B13]
"Noggo," 26 March 1958. [B6]
"Out of All Possible Times,"
    n.d. [B7]
"Seal," n.d. [B9]
"Speak No More," 14 January 1958.
    [B2]
"Then Look behind You," n.d.
    [B4]

6. LONGER FICTION

"Across the River." [A211]
Alien Art. [A189]
Alien from Arcturus. [A55]
Alien Way. [A146]
"Ancient, My Enemy." [A171]
"Breakdown."
"Brothers." [A190]
"The Case of the Stalking
    Monster."
Combat SF. [A203]
Danger--Human. [A172]
"Dicker."
Dorsai! [A96]
Double World (Delusion World?).
    [A112]
The Dragon and the George. [A206]
"The Earth Shakers."
"Earthman" ("The Man from
    Earth"?). [A143]
The Far Call. [A194]
Five Fates. [See A176]

"Goblin Passage."
Gordon R. Dickson's Science
    Fiction Best. [A216]
Gremlins, Go Home! [A195]
"Grizzly Gold."
"The Half-Pint Posted." [A95]
Home from the Shore. [A137]
Hour of the Horde. [A169]
"The Law Twister" ("The Law-
    Twister Shorty"). [A180]
Life Boat. [A200]
"Line Team" ("Building on the
    Line"?). [A164]
"The Love Song."
Mission to Universe. [A152]
"The Mortal and the Monster."
    [A208]
"Muscle Jimmy."
Mutants. [A173]
Naked to the Stars. [A123]
"Natural Advantage."
Necromancer. [A128]
"No Place to Lie Down."
None but Man. [A165]
The Outposter. [A182]
"Perfectly Adjusted." [A48]
Planet Run. [A160]
The Pritcher Mass. [A187]
Pro. [A204]
"Quarantine."
The R-Master. [A191]
Secret under Antarctica. [A134]
Secret under the Caribbean. [A141]
"Secret under the Mediterranean."
"Secret under the Reef."
Secret under the Sea. [A101]
"The Sixth Witness."
Sleepwalker's World. [A183]
Soldier, Ask Not. [A163]
Spacepaw. [A167]
The Space Swimmers. [A162]
Space Winners. [A154]
Star Prince Charlie. [A201]
The Star Road. [A192]
"Starship Master."
Tactics of Mistake. [A178]
"Things Which Are Caesar's."
    [A185]
Three to Dorsai! [A205]
"Time Fault." [? cf. A213]
Time Storm. [A213]

"Twig." [A197]   "A Wobble in Wockii Futures."
"Wanderers of Outworld."   [A147]
"The White Cure."   "Wolf by the Ears."
"When among Humanoids."   Wolfling. [A166]

    In addition to the short stories, fragments, novels, novelettes,
collections, and anthologies listed, the Dickson Papers include materials relating to such miscellaneous writings as Dickson's articles;
various materials relating to Dickson's extracurricular activities
(e.g., membership in the MFA); materials for an untitled novel; miscellaneous notes (which could not be assigned to a particular title);
and materials relating to Dickson's college days (including miscellaneous notes for stories).

B: Chronological Checklist of Novels, Collections, and Anthologies by Dickson

1956 Alien from Arcturus (Arcturus Landing) [A55]; Mankind on the Run (On the Run) [A56].
1957 Earthman's Burden [A62].
1960 The Genetic General (Dorsai!) [A100]; Secret under the Sea [A101]; Time to Teleport [A102].
1961 Delusion World [A112]; Spacial Delivery [A113], Naked to the Stars [A124].
1962 Necromancer (No Room for Man) [A128].
1963 Secret under Antarctica [A134]; Rod Serling's Triple W: Witches, Warlocks and Werewolves [A138].
1964 Secret under the Caribbean [A141].
1965 The Alien Way [A146]; Space Winners [A154]; Mission to Universe [A152].
1967 Planet Run [A160]; Rod Serling's Devils and Demons [A161]; The Space Swimmers [A162]; Soldier, Ask Not [A163].
1969 None but Man [A165]; Spacepaw [A167]; Wolfling [A168].
1970 Danger--Human (The Book of Gordon R. Dickson) [A172]; Mutants [A173]; Hour of the Horde [A177].
1971 The Tactics of Mistake [A181]; Sleepwalker's World [A183].
1972 The Outposter [A184]; The Pritcher Mass [A188].
1973 Alien Art [A189]; The R-Master [A191]; The Star Road [A192].
1974 Gremlins, Go Home! [A195]; Ancient, My Enemy [A198].
1975 Star Prince Charlie [A201]; Combat SF [A203]; Three to Dorsai! [A205].
1976 The Dragon and the George [A206]; The Lifeship (Lifeboat) [A207].
1977 Time Storm [A213].
1978 The Far Call [A214]; Nebula Winners Twelve [A215]; Gordon R. Dickson's SF Best (A216); Home from the Shore [A217]; Pro [A219].
1979 Masters of Everon [A220]; The Spirit of Dorsai [A223].
1980 Lost Dorsai [A228]; In Iron Years [A229].
1981 Love Not Human [A230].

51 books: 36 novels, 10 collections, 5 anthologies

C: Series by Dickson

1. The Childe Cycle
    (a) Completed novels
    Dorsai! (The Genetic General), 1959 [A96].
    Necromancer (None but Man), 1962 [A128].
    Soldier, Ask Not, 1967 [A163].
    The Tactics of Mistake, 1970 [A178].
    (b) Projected novels
    The Final Encyclopedia.
    Childe.
    (c) Illuminations of the cycle
    "Warrior," 1965 [A157].
    "Brothers," 1973 [A190].
    "Amanda Morgan," 1979 [A222].
    "Lost Dorsai," 1980 [A225].
    (d) Extracts from the cycle
    "Soldier, Ask Not," 1964 [A145].
    "The Final Encyclopedia: An Excerpt," 1980 [A227].
    (e) Collections with original connecting material
    Three to Dorsai! 1975 [A205]
    The Spirit of Dorsai, 1979 [A223].
    (f) Dorsai stories outside the cycle
    "Lulungomeena," 1954 [A34].
    "Act of Creation," 1957 [A68].

2. Dilbian series
    "The Man in the Mailbag," 1960 [A95].
    Spacial Delivery, 1961 [A113].
    Spacepaw 1969 [A167].
    "The Law-Twister Shorty," 1971 [A180].

3. Shane Everts series
    "Enter a Pilgrim," 1974 [A196].
    "The Cloak and the Staff," 1980 [A226].

4. Robby Hoenig series
    Secret under the Sea, 1960 [A101].
    Secret under Antarctica, 1963 [A134].

Secret under the Caribbean, 1964 [A141].

5. Tom and Lucy Parent series
   "Rex and Mr. Rejilla," 1958 [A80].
   "Who Dares a Bulbur Eat?" 1962 [A132].
   "The Faithful Wilf," 1963 [A139].
   "A Wobble in Wockii Futures," 1965 [A147].

6. Hank Shallo, World Scout, series
   "Sleight of Wit," 1961 [A125].
   "Soupstone," 1965 [A148].
   "Catch a Tartar," 1965 [A150].

7. Hoka series, with Poul Anderson.
   *"The Sheriff of Canyon Gulch" ("Heroes Are Made"), 1951 [A9].
   *"In Hoka Signo Vinces," 1953 [A26].
   *"The Adventure of the Misplaced Hound," 1953 [A32].
   *"Yo Ho Hoka!" 1955 [A45].
   *"The Tiddlywink Warriors," 1955 [A50].
   "Joy in Mudville," 1955 [A52].
   *"Don Jones," 1957 [A61].
   "Undiplomatic Immunity," 1957 [A69].
   "Full Pack" ("Hokas Wild"), 1957 [A73].
   Star Prince Charlie, 1975 [A201].

*Collected in Earthman's Burden, 1957 [A62].

D: Translations of Dickson's Works

The confusion over translations has prompted many despairing complaints from science fiction authors, as the pages of SFWA Bulletin testify. Few have any but the vaguest idea how much of their fiction has been translated: rarely do they see royalties or even receive complimentary copies of publications of their short stories, though the situation is better where novels are concerned. Checking for translations poses particular difficulties for the researcher, since so few are to be found in North America. The best collection is held by the MIT Science Fiction Society in Boston, Massachusetts. Gordon Dickson has many translations of his novels in his private collection.

What follows is a list, by language, of the translations I was able to find, though not always verify. It can be but partial, given the special difficulties attending such a task (e.g., foreign editions of some magazines appear in several languages, but contents are not necessarily identical). Nevertheless, the listing does give an indication of the extent to which Dickson's works have been translated.

1. DUTCH

"Sleight of Wit." As "Kunstgreep." In Science-fictionverhalen 5.
    Utrecht and Antwerp: Prisma-Boeken, 1966 [paper]. [A125]

"Computers Don't Argue." In De Speekselboom. Laren, North Holland:
    Uitgeverij Luitingh, 1975. [Note: Collection of some of the
    stories in Damon Knight, ed., Nebula Award Stories 1965.] [A151]

"Enter a Pilgrim." In Verloren Groene Droom. Utrecht and Antwerp:
    Uitgeverij Het Spectrum, 1978. [A196]

Appendix D

2. FRENCH

*"Zeepsday." As "La semaine de huit jours." Fiction, no. 51. [A58]

*"Rescue Mission." Fiction. [A64]

*"St. Dragon and the George." Fiction. [A72]

"The Christmas Present." As "Noël sur Cidor." Fiction, no. 73
    (December 1959):46-53. [A79]

*"A Matter of Technique." As "Simple affaire de technique." Fiction,
    no. 61. [A82]

"Brother Charlie." As "Opération Grand Frère." Fiction, no. 124
    (March 1964):5-33. [A84]

"The Amulet." As "Le remplaçant." Fiction, no. 136 (March 1965):
    93-108. [A93]

Dorsai! As Dorsai. Paris: Editions OPTA, 1971 [paper]. [A96]

"Rehabilitated." As "L'apprentissage." Fiction, no. 135 (February
    1965):92-104. [A114]

"A Taste of Tenure." As "Les inamovibles." Galaxie, no. 78
    (November 1970):60-86. [A119]

"The Haunted Village." As "Le village hanté." Fiction, no. 112
    (March 1963):75-91. [A121]

Necromancer. As Necromant. Paris: Editions OPTA, 1974 [paper].
    [A128]

"Roofs of Silver." As "Les toits d'argent." Fiction, no. 121
    (December 1963):73-97. [A133]

"Soldier, Ask Not." As "Pour quelle guerre . . ." Galaxie, no. 42
    (October 1967):4-60. [A145]

"An Ounce of Emotion." As "La machine à tuer la guerre." Galaxie,
    no. 46 (February 1968):68-92. [A153]

Soldier, Ask Not. As Pour quelle guerre . . . Paris: Editions OPTA,
    1972 [paper]. [A163]

The Tactics of Mistake. As La stratégie de l'erreur. Paris:
    Editions OPTA, 1973 [paper]. [A178]

The Pritcher Mass. As La Masse Pritcher. Paris: Editions Albin
    Michel, 1979 [paper]. [A187]

Appendix D

3. GERMAN

"Tresspass!" As "Ein Tempel als Reisegepäck." Utopia-Magazin, no.
    22:68-85. [A7]

"The Friendly Man." As "Am Ende der Zeit." Terra Nova Science
    Fiction, no. 78:20-29. [A8]

"The Error of Their Ways." As "Der rechte Weg." Terra Nova Science
    Fiction, no. 78:30-41. [A10]

*"The Mousetrap." As "Die Mausefall." Galaxis, no. 8. [A18]

*"Lulungomeena." As "Lulungomeena," Galaxis, no. 15. [A34]

"The Queer Critter." As "Das Seltsame Wesen." Utopia Zukunftsroman,
    no. 474:52-54. [A41]

Alien from Arcturus. As Der Fremde vom Arcturus. Terra: Utopische
    Romane Science Fiction, no. 341, 1957 [paper]. [A55]

Mankind on the Run. As Hetzjagd im All. Terra-Extra, no. 58, 1965
    [paper]. [A56]

Earthman's Burden. As Alexander Jones--Diplomat der Erde. 2 vols.
    Terra: Utopische Romane Science Fiction, nos. 382-83, 1965
    [paper]. [A62]

"Danger--Human!" As "Vorsicht--Mensch!" Terra Nova Science Fiction,
    no. 78:5-19. [A77]

*"Brother Charlie." As "Projekt 'Grosser Bruder.'" Heyne SF-
    Zaschenbuch, no. 3048. [A84]

The Genetic General. As Söldner der Galaxis. Munich: Moewig-Verlag,
    1970 [paper]. [A100]

*"Button, Button." As "Knopfdrucker." Heyne SF-Zaschenbuch, no. 3056.
    [A109]

*Delusion World. As Planet der Phantome. Terra: Utopische Romane
    Science Fiction, no. 249, 1962. [A112]

*Spacial Delivery. As Regierungspost für Dilbia. Terra: Utopische
    Romane Science Fiction, no. 260, 1963. [A113]

"Rehabilitated." As "Die Unvollkommenen." In Saturn im Morgenlicht.
    Munich: Heyne, 1963, pp. 123-41 [paper]. [A114]

Naked to the Stars. As Gewalt zwischen den Sternen. Hamburg:
    Winther, 1967. [A123]

"Sleight of Wit." As "Die ultimate Waffe." Terra Nova Science
  Fiction, no. 78:41-52. [A125]

"Idiot Solvant." As "Das Versuchskaninchen." Terra Nova Science
  Fiction, no. 78:52-65. [A126]

*Necromancer. As Nichts für Menschen. Munich: Heyne, 1979. [A128]

The Alien Way. As Die Fremden. Munich: König, 1973 [paper]. [A146]

"Computers Don't Argue." As "Computer streiten nicht." In Computer
  Streiten Nicht. Munich: Lichtenberg, 1970. [Note: Collection
  of some of the stories in Damon Knight, ed., Nebula Award Stories
  1965.] [A151]

  Dolly Dolittle's Crime Club 3. Zurich: Diogenes, 1973 [paper].
    [A151]
  Ruth J. Kilchenmann, ed. Schaue Kisten Machen Geschichten.
    Nordlingen: IBM Deutschland, 1977. [A151]

Mission to Universe. As Mission im Universum. Terra: Utopische
  Romane Science Fiction, no. 500, 1967. [A152]

The Space Swimmers. As Weltraum-schwimmer. Rastatt and Baden:
  Erich Pabel, 1978 [paper]. [A162]

Wolfling. As Im galaktischen Reich. Rastatt and Baden: Erich Pabel,
  1973. [A166]

  *Munich: Moewig, 1973 [paper]. [A166]

Spacepaw. As Der Agent. Rastatt and Baden: Erich Pabel, 1978
  [paper]. [A167]

  *Munich: Moewig, 1978 [paper]. [A167]

Danger--Human. As Vorsicht--Mensch! Rastatt and Baden: Erich Pabel,
  1972. [A172]

  *Munich: Moewig, 1972 [paper]. [A172]

"Walker between the Planes." As "Einzelgänger." In Der Zwischenbereich
  [Five Fates]. Munich: Heyne, 1975 [paper]. [A175]

The Tactics of Mistake. As Das Planeten-Duel. Rastatt and Baden:
  Erich Pabel, 1975. [A178]

  *Munich: Moewig, 1975 [paper]. [A178]

"Jean Duprès." In Nova: eine Anthologie [Nova 1]. Bergisch
  Gladbach: Bastei-Lubbe, 1973 [paper]. [A179]

Appendix D

The Outposter. As Pioniere des Kosmos. Rastatt and Baden: Erich
    Pabel, 1973 [paper]. [A182]

    *Munich: Moewig, 1973 [paper]. [A182]

Sleepwalker's World. As Geschöpfe der Nacht. Rastatt and Baden:
    Erich Pabel, 1972 [paper]. [A183]

    *Munich: Moewig, 1972 [paper]. [A183]

The Pritcher Mass. As Das Millionen-Bewusstsein. Rastatt and Baden:
    Erich Pabel, 1975 [paper]. [A187]

    *Munich: Moewig, 1975 [paper]. [A187]

*Alien Art. As Charlies Planet. Munich: Moewig, 1975. [A189]

The R-Master. As Utopia 2050. Rastatt and Baden: Erich Pabel, 1976
    [paper]. [A191]

    *Munich: Moewig, 1976 [paper]. [A191]

*The Far Call. As Der ferne Ruf. Munich: Heyne, 1979. [A194]

*Ancient, My Enemy. As Uralt, Mein Feind. Munich: Heyne, 1979 [A198]

*The Lifeboat. As Kurs auf 20B-40. Munich: Goldmann, 1976. [A200]

*The Dragon and the George. As Die Nacht der Drachen. Munich: Heyne,
    1980. [A206]

*Masters of Everon. As Herren von Everon. Munich: Moewig, 1980.
    [A220]

4. ITALIAN

"The Sheriff of Canyon Gulch." As "Lo sceriffo di Canyon Gulch."
    Fantastrenna Urania, no. 363 (December 1964):4-33. [A9]

*"Time Grabber." As "Documenti sul caso della Cronobenna." Gamma,
    no. 15 (February 1967). [A21]

"In Hoka Signo Vinces." As "In Hoka signo vinces." Fantastrenna
    Urania, no. 363 (December 1964):34-63. [A26]

"The Adventure of the Misplaced Hound." As "Hoka Holmes."
    Fantastrenna Urania, no. 63 (December 1964):64-98. [A32]

Mankind on the Run. As La razza senza fine. Urania, no. 204 (May
    1959):3-116. [A56]

Appendix D

*"Brother Charlie." As "Fratello Charlie." Fantasia & Fantascienza, no. 10 (October 1963). [A84]

"The Man in the Mailbag." As "L'uomo nella Borsa della Posta." Galaxy 4 (June 1961):85-119. [A95]

The Genetic General. As Il mercanario di Dorsai. Galassia Romanzi di Fantascienza, no. 23 (November-December 1962). [A100]

As Generale Genetico. Milan: Editrice Nord, 1974. [A100]

"The Hours Are Good." As "Il momento propizio." Galaxy 5 (September 1962):66-79. [A110]

"An Honorable Death." As "Una morte onorevole." Galaxy 6 (May 1963): 83-104. [A115]

Naked to the Stars. As La missione del tenente Truant. Milan: Arnoldo Mondadori, 1964. [A123]

"Napoleon's Skullcap." As "Il Cappello di Napoleone." Fantasia & Fantascienza, no. 9 (September 1963):61-83. [A127]

Necromancer. As Negromante. Milan: Editrice Nord, 1973. [A128]

*"Three-Part Puzzle." As "Un problema di traduzione." Urania, no. 348 (6 September 1964). [A129]

"Who Dares a Bulbur Eat?" As "Chi Affronta un Piatto Bulbur?" Galaxy 6 (October 1963):84-102. [A132]

*"Roofs of Silver." As "Tetti d'argento." Fantasia & Fantascienza, no. 5 (April 1963). [A133]

Secret under Antarctica. As Spionaggio nell' Antartide. Milan: Valentino Bompiani, 1968 [paper]. [A134]

"Home from the Shore." As "Nati Dall'Abisso." Galaxy 7 (February 1964):3-50. [A137]

*"The Faithful Wilf." As "La fedele Wilf." Galaxy 7 (April 1964). [A139]

"The Man from Earth." As "Il Terrestre." Urania, no. 344 (9 August 1964):107-20. [A143]

"On Messenger Mountain." As "K.94 Chiama Terra." Urania, no. 368 (24 January 1965). [A144]

The Alien Way. As Esche Nello Spazio. Milan: Editrice Nord, 1971. [A146]

"Computers Don't Argue." As "Coi computer non si discute." Robot: Rivista di Fantascienza, no. 4 (July 1976):27–40. [A151]

"An Ounce of Emotion." As "La guerra, la pace, e annie." Urania, no. 416 (December 1965):85–109. [A153]

Soldier, Ask Not. As Soldato non Chiedere. Milan: Editrice Nord, 1973. [A163]

Spacepaw. As L'Artiglio dello Spazio. Rome: Fanucci, 1972 [paper]. [A167]

The Tactics of Mistake. As Tattica dell'errore. Milan: Editrice Nord, 1972. [A178]

The Outposter. As Lo Spaziale. Milan: Arnoldo Mondadori, 1974 [paper]. [A182]

Sleepwalker's World. As Il Mondo dei Sonnambuli. Milan: Omega SF, 1977. [A183]

"Things Which Are Caesar's." As "Quel che è di Cesare." In Quando il sole si Fermo [The Day the Sun Stood Still]. Varese: dall'Oglio, 1973. [A185]

"Twig." As "Twig." In Stellar [Stellar 1]. Milan: Longanesi, 1977. [A197]

The Lifeboat. As Astroincendio Doloso. Milan: Arnoldo Mondadori, 1977 [paper]. [A200]

5. JAPANESE

"Joy in Mudville." In Japanese edition of FSF. [A52]

Earthman's Burden. 1972. [A62]

"With Butter and Mustard." In Japanese edition of FSF. [A78]

"A Matter of Technique." In Japanese edition of FSF. [A82]

Secret under the Sea. 1972. [Also version in comic format in Shonen Gaho (June 1961), 2 vols.] [A101]

Space Winners. 1971. [A154]

"Warrior." In Japanese translation of Judith Merril, ed., 11th Annual Edition: The Year's Best S-F. [A157]

Appendix D

6. PORTUGUESE

Dorsai! As O General Do Universo. Alferragide: Editorial Panorama, n.d. [paper]. [A96]

7. SPANISH

* Time to Teleport. As La era del teleporte. Cenit: 71, 1964. [A102]

"Sleight of Wit." As "Rasgio de Ingenio." In Antología De Nonvelas de Anticipación (Primera Selección). Edited by Ana Mª Perales. Barcelona: Ediciones Acervo, 1963, pp. 203-23. [A125]

The Alien Way. As Al estilo extraterrestre. Barcelona: Ediciones Martínez Roca, 1977. [A146]

Gremlins, Go Home! As No mas duendes. Buenos Aires: Ediciones Lidiun, 1978 [paper]. [A195]

8. SWEDISH

"Rehabilitated." As "Rehabiliterad." Häpna Science Fiction Tidskrift, nos. 7-8 (1963):69-84. [A114]

E: Reviews Excluded

The following reviews have been excluded from Part D, "Critical Studies," because they are too brief or nonevaluative.

ANON. Review of Space Winners. Spectator, 2 June 1967, p. 656.

ANON. Review of Danger--Human. Top of the News 26 (June 1970):427.

ANON. Review of The Tactics of Mistake. American Book Collector 21 (May 1971):4.

ANON. Review of Mutants. Kliatt Paperback Book Guide 7 (November 1973):23.

ANON. Review of Mutants. Vertex [fanzine] 1 (December 1973):11.

ANON. Review of Ancient, My Enemy. PW, 5 August 1974, p. 53.

ANON. Review of Ancient, My Enemy. PW, 15 March 1976, p. 59.

ANON. Review of Dorsai! Book Week, 24 February 1980, p. 13.

ANON. Review of The Spirit of Dorsai. School Library Journal 26 (April 1980):136.

BROWN, C. Review of Star Road. Locus [fanzine], 23 October 1974, p. 4.

_____. Review of Ancient, My Enemy, Dorsai!, Soldier, Ask Not, and Three to Dorsai! Locus [fanzine], 30 June 1976, p. 6.

COGSWELL, THEODORE R. "A World Full of 'Sleepwalkers.'" Minneapolis Sunday Tribune, 15 August 1971.

Appendix E

ROBINSON, SPIDER. Review of Soldier, Ask Not. Galaxy 37 (July 1976): 123-24.

_____. Review of The Book of Gordon R. Dickson. Galaxy 37 (November 1976):151-52.

_____. Review of Ancient, My Enemy. Galaxy 37 (December 1976):129.

_____. Review of Gordon R. Dickson's SF Best. ASF 98 (June 1978): 168.

The following reviews have been omitted because information on them arrived too late for inclusion.

ANON. Review of Star Prince Charlie. KR 43 (15 April 1975):452.

ANON. Review of Star Prince Charlie. Booklist 71 (1 June 1975):1009.

BROWN, CHARLES. Review of Star Prince Charlie. Locus [fanzine], 3 June 1975, p. 2.

HAYNES, E. Review of Star Prince Charlie. School Library Journal 22 (September 1975):94.

Indexes

Published Works of
Gordon R. Dickson

Criticism and Interviews

A., R.G.
-Review of <u>Alien Art</u>, D210
-Review of <u>The Dragon and</u>
   <u>the George</u>, D201
"About Gordon R. Dickson,"
   Sandra Miesel, D222
"Ad Astra!" Bruce Kvam, D221
Afterword to <u>Home from the Shore</u>,
   Sandra Miesel, D223
Anderson, Poul, "In Re: Gordon
   R. Dickson," D110

Badami, Mary Kenny, "A Feminist
   Critique of Science Fiction,"
   D168
Banks, Michael A.
   -"SF Prediction: Speculation
   or Future Facts?" C56
   -"Short Interview with
   Gordon R. Dickson, A," C42
Bell, Thomas R., Review of <u>The</u>
   <u>Tactics of Mistake</u>, D75
Berman, Ruth, "Division Mars
   Dickson Story" [Review of
   <u>The Outposter</u>], D94
Bester, Alfred, Review of <u>The</u>
   <u>Genetic General</u>, D12
"Biolog: Gordon R. Dickson,"
   Jay Kay Klein, D247
Birlem, Lynne M., Review of <u>The</u>
   <u>Lifeship</u>, D169
Blish, James
   -Review of "Jean Duprès," D58
   -Review of <u>Sleepwalker's</u>
   <u>World</u>, D95
   -Review of <u>The Tactics of</u>
   <u>Mistake</u>, D96

Blishen, Edward, "Children's Books:
   For the Almost Old" [Review of
   <u>Space Winners</u>], D37
Boatwright, Taliaferro, "Getting
   Along Swimmingly" [Review of
   <u>Secret under the Caribbean</u>],
   D27
Bodart, Joni, Review of <u>Combat SF</u>,
   D146
Boucher, Anthony
   -Review of <u>Alien from</u>
      <u>Arcturus</u>, D2
   -Review of <u>Earthman's Burden</u>,
      D7
   -Review of <u>Mankind on the</u>
      <u>Run</u>, D3
Brady, Mary Lou, Review of
   <u>Gremlins, Go Home!</u> D129
Brodsky, Allyn B., Review of <u>The</u>
   <u>R-Master</u>, D147
Brown, Charles
   -Review of <u>Combat SF</u> and
      <u>The R-Master</u>, D148
   -Review of <u>The Far Call</u>, D211
   -Review of <u>Home from the Shore</u>
      and <u>Pro</u>, D233
   -Review of <u>Sleepwalker's</u>
      <u>World</u>, D149
   -Review of <u>Time Storm</u>, D212
Budrys, Algis
   -Review of <u>The Dragon and the</u>
      <u>George</u>, D202
   -Review of <u>Pro</u>, D234
   -Review of <u>The Tactics of</u>
      <u>Mistake</u>, D76
Burk, J., Review of <u>Combat SF</u>,
   D150

101

Burns, S., Review of The Star
Road, D151

Calvallini, Jean, Review of
Danger--Human, D59
Carper, Steve, Review of The
Pritcher Mass, D203
Childe Cycle. See also indi-
vidual titles listed in
Appendix C1; entries C17,
C22, C30, C36, C38, C52,
C55, C58
-Dalmyn, Tony, "The Prince
among the Planets:
Machiavelli and Gordon R.
Dickson," D153
-Klein, Jay Kay, "The Dorsai
Irregulars," D248
-McMurray, Clifford, "The
Different Man: Dickson's
Donal Graeme," D236
-Miesel, Sandra
--"About Gordon R.
Dickson," D222
--"The Plume and the
Sword," D249
--"The Road to the Dark
Tower," D251
-O'Reilly, Timothy, "The
Childe Cycle," D239
-Thompson, Raymond H., "Shai
Dorsai! A Study of the
Hero Figure in Gordon R.
Dickson's Dorsai!" D240
"Childe Cycle, The," Timothy
O'Reilly, D239
"Children's Books: For the
Almost Old" [Review of Space
Winners], Edward Blishen,
D37
Clute, John, Review of The
Lifeship, D204
Conan, Neal J., Review of Combat
SF, D152
Connelly, Wayne
-Review of Spacepaw, D60
-". . . Whose Game Was
Empires" [Review of The
Tactics of Mistake], D97
"Conquered World, A" [Review of
Space Winners], D35

Cotts, S.E., "The Spectroscope."
Review of The Genetic General,
D13
Cross, Michael S., Review of The
Lifeship, D170

Dalmyn, Tony, "The Prince among
the Planets: Machiavelli and
Gordon R. Dickson," D153
D'Ammassa, Don
-Review of Ancient, My Enemy,
D171
-Review of The R-Master, D130
Davidson, Avram, Review of The
Pritcher Mass, D111
Davis, Monte, Review of Spacepaw,
D172
del Rey, Lester
-Review of Dorsai! D173
-Review of The Far Call, D214
-Review of The Outposter, D98
-Review of The Pritcher Mass,
D112
-Review of The Tactics of
Mistake, D77
-Review of Three to Dorsai!
D174
-Review of Time Storm, D213
"Dickson, Gordon R(upert),"
Donald H. Tuck, D141
"Different Man: Dickson's Donal
Graeme, The," Clifford
McMurray, D236
"Division Mars Dickson Story"
[Review of The Outposter],
Ruth Berman, D94
"Dorsai Irregulars, The," Jay Kay
Klein, D248

Easton, Tom, Review of Home from
the Shore and The Spirit of
Dorsai, D242
Ellison, Harlan, Review of Mutants,
D78
Evans, Chris, Review of None but
Man, D215

"Feminist Critique of Science
Fiction, A," Mary Kenny
Badami, D168
Foreword to Gordon R. Dickson's

Kemske, Floyd, Review of <u>Time Storm</u>, D220
King, Tappan
   -Review of <u>The Lifeship</u>, D185
   -Review of <u>Star Prince Charlie</u>, D186
Klein, Jay Kay
   -"Biolog: Gordon R. Dickson," D247
   -"The Dorsai Irregulars," D248
Knight, Damon
   -"Infinity's Choice" [Review of <u>Alien from Arcturus</u>], D4
   -Review of <u>Earthman's Burden</u>, D9
Kvam, Bruce, "Ad Astra!" D221

Laite, Berkley, Review of <u>Danger --Human</u>, D62
Lambe, Dean R., Review of <u>The Spirit of Dorsai</u> and <u>Home from the Shore</u>, D235
Lampton, C., Review of <u>The R-Master</u>, D134
Livingstone, Dennis, Review of <u>The Lifeship</u>, D179
Lundquist, Barb, "For Gordon R. Dickson, Responsibility, Fantasy Join in Science Fiction," C40

McCauley, Kirby, Review of <u>The R-Master</u>, D135
McGuire, Paul, "Yes, but How Much Do They Weigh?" [Review of <u>Gremlins, Go Home!</u>], D180
McMurray, Clifford R.
   -"The Different Man: Dickson's Donal Graeme," D236
   -"An Interview with Gordon R. Dickson," C55
   -Review of <u>Ancient, My Enemy</u>, D181
   -Review of <u>Gordon R. Dickson's SF Best</u>, D237
   -Review of <u>Soldier, Ask Not</u>, D182
   -Review of <u>Three to Dorsai!</u>

D183
MacPherson, W.N.
   -Review of <u>Dorsai!</u> D184
   -Review of <u>Soldier, Ask Not</u>, D156
MacVicar, William, "They Don't Sniff at Science Fiction Writers Now," C34
Madsen, Alan, "In the Future Tense" [Review of <u>Space Winners</u>], D31
Martin, D.R., "Conversations with Three Who Write 'Sci-Fi': Frederik Pohl, Clifford D. Simak, and Gordon R. Dickson Talk about Their Work," C57
Mattern, P., Review of <u>The Pritcher Mass</u>, D136
Meacham, Beth
   -Review of <u>The Lifeship</u>, D185
   -Review of <u>Star Prince Charlie</u>, D186
Merril, Judith
   -Review of <u>The Alien Way</u>, D28
   -Review of <u>Mission to Universe</u>, D32
"MFS Members as Seen by Squanchfoot," D1
Michalik, Anne P., Review of <u>Hour of the Horde</u>, D63
Miesel, Sandra
   -"About Gordon R. Dickson," D222
   -Afterword to <u>Home from the Shore</u>, D223
   -"<u>Algol</u> Interview: Gordon R. Dickson," C52
   -"A Conversation with Gordon R. Dickson," C58
   -"The Plume and the Sword," D249
   -Review of <u>The Far Call</u>, D238
   -Review of <u>The Spirit of Dorsai</u>, D250
   -"The Road to the Dark Tower," D251
Miller, Dan
   -Review of <u>Combat SF</u>, D157
   -Review of <u>The Dragon and the George</u>, D206
   -Review of <u>The Lifeship</u>, D187,

D153

Rapkin, J., Review of <u>None but</u>
<u>Man</u>, D67
Reviews
  -<u>Alien Art</u>, D102, D103, D115,
    D138, D210, D226
  -<u>Alien from Arcturus</u>, D2,
    D4, D5
  -<u>Alien Way, The</u>, D28
  -<u>Ancient, My Enemy</u>, D123,
    D133, D143, D160, D171,
    D181, D194
  -<u>Combat SF</u>, D144, D146, D148,
    D150, D152, D155, D157,
    D158, D161, D162, D189
  -<u>Danger--Human</u>, D42, D43,
    D53, D59, D62, D69, D85
  -<u>Delusion World</u>, D19
  -<u>Dorsai!</u> D173, D184, D196
  -<u>Dragon and the George, The</u>,
    D163, D176, D190, D195,
    D197, D201, D202, D206
  -<u>Earthman's Burden</u>, D7, D8,
    D9, D10, D11, D65, D253
  -<u>Far Call, The</u>, D207, D208,
    D211, D214, D230, D238
  -<u>The Genetic General</u>, D12,
    D13, D14, D17
  -<u>Gordon R. Dickson's SF Best</u>,
    D237
  -<u>Gremlins, Go Home!</u> D124,
    D125, D126, D129, D180
  -<u>Home from the Shore</u>, D233,
    D235, D242
  -<u>Hour of the Horde</u>, D54, D55,
    D63, D68, D86
  -"<u>Jean Duprès</u>," D58, D79
  -<u>Lifeship, The</u>, D164, D165,
    D169, D170, D175, D178,
    D179, D185, D187, D188,
    D193, D204
  -<u>Lost Dorsai</u>, D244
  -<u>Mankind on the Run</u>, D3, D6
  -<u>Mission to Universe</u>, D32
  -"<u>Mortal and the Monster</u>,
    The," D167
  -<u>Mutants</u>, D56, D57, D66, D78,
    D81, D84, D131
  -<u>Naked to the Stars</u>, D18,
    D20, D166

  -<u>Nebula Winners Twelve</u>, D224,
    D228, D231
  -<u>Necromancer</u>, D21, D23
  -<u>None but Man</u>, D44, D45, D46,
    D50, D52, D61, D67, D215
  -<u>Outposter, The</u>, D89, D90,
    D94, D98, D100, D104, D116
  -<u>Planet Run</u>, D38
  -<u>Pritcher Mass, The</u>, D91, D92,
    D99, D105, D111, D112,
    D117, D119, D121, D136,
    D203
  -<u>Pro</u>, D233, D234, D241
  -<u>R-Master, The</u>, D106, D107,
    D127, D128, D130, D132,
    D134, D135, D142, D147,
    D148, D154, D159, D178,
    D179
  -<u>Secret under Antarctica</u>,
    D24, D25
  -<u>Secret under the Caribbean</u>,
    D27
  -<u>Secret under the Sea</u>, D15,
    D16, D22
  -<u>Sleepwalker's World</u>, D70,
    D71, D72, D82, D88, D93,
    D95, D101, D120, D139,
    D149
  -<u>Soldier, Ask Not</u>, D36, D40,
    D145, D156, D182
  -<u>Spacepaw</u>, D47, D49, D51,
    D60, D64, D80, D172, D191
  -<u>Space Swimmers, The</u>, D39, D41
  -<u>Space Winners</u>, D26, D29, D30,
    D31, D33, D34, D35, D37
  -<u>Spacial Delivery</u>, D19
  -<u>Spirit of Dorsai, The</u>, D235,
    D242, D245, D250, D252
  -<u>Star Prince Charlie</u>, D177,
    D186, D192, D198
  -<u>Star Road, The</u>, D108, D109,
    D114, D122, D137, D140,
    D151
  -<u>Tactics of Mistake, The</u>,
    D73, D74, D75, D76, D77,
    D83, D87, D96, D97, D113
  -<u>Three to Dorsai!</u> D174, D183
  -<u>Time Storm</u>, D199, D200, D205,
    D209, D212, D213, D218,
    D219, D229, D232
  -<u>Time to Teleport</u>, D14, D17

Copyediting directed by Ara Salibian.
Text formatted and produced by Fred Welden.
Camera-ready copy typed by Ann Condon
          on an IBM Selectric.
Printed and bound by Braun-Brumfield, Inc.,
          of Ann Arbor, Michigan.